LAW VERSUS POWER

LAW VERSUS POWER

OUR GLOBAL FIGHT FOR HUMAN RIGHTS

WOLFGANG KALECK
TRANSLATED BY FIONA NELSON

OR Books

New York · London

© 2015 Carl Hanser Verlag GmbH & Co. KG, München
English translation © 2018 Fiona Nelson. Original title: *Mit Recht gegen die Macht.*

Published by OR Books, New York and London

All rights information: rights@orbooks.com
Visit our website at www.orbooks.com

First printing 2018

Library of Congress Cataloging-in-Publication Data: A catalog record for this book is available from the Library of Congress.
British Library Cataloging in Publication Data: A catalog record for this book is available from the British Library.

Typeset by Lapiz Digital Services. Printed by BookMobile, USA, and CPI, UK.

paperback ISBN 978-1-68219-173-6 • ebook ISBN 978-1-68219-174-3

And his friend said yes, of course he would, straight away, and then: What's that sound? Are you crying? And The Eye said yes, he couldn't stop crying, he didn't know what was happening to him, he had been crying for hours. His French friend told him to calm down. At this The Eye, still crying, laughed, said he would do that and hung up. But he went on crying, and couldn't stop.

Roberto Bolaño, "Mauricio ('The Eye') Silva"

Dear God, spare me from living in uninteresting times.

Executioner Völpel in Thomas Brasch's Engel aus Eisen

CONTENTS

FOREWORD

Edward Snowden

I met Wolfgang Kaleck in January of 2014 when he visited me for the first time in Moscow. During that visit, and in many subsequent visits and conversations since, I came to appreciate that Wolfgang combines a lawyer's attention to detail, a radical's view of power, and an activist's vision for a better world.

I came forward in 2013 because I had observed, during a decade in the US intelligence community, that people in positions of power enjoyed complete impunity for grave violations of the Constitution and human rights, even as those with the least power were held to the highest standards of accountability and retribution. Wolfgang has devoted his entire career to reversing this state of affairs—defending the victims of torture and other grave human rights abuses, while working to shrink the world for their torturers.

Even as I write this, the US Senate has just confirmed a central player in the Bush administration's torture regime as the next director of the CIA. At moments like this, it can be tempting to throw up our collective hands in disgust and resignation and to wonder whether we should do something else with our lives. Wolfgang has helped me to fight against these feelings of hopelessness. His combination of patience and persistence is a model for all of us who take on causes whose success is measured in generations, not in months or even years.

General Pinochet did not expect to spend his twilight years being chased around the world by courageous lawyers and victims. Donald Rumsfeld should not assume that he will escape the same fate.

And when that day arrives—when the history of our era is written not by the torturers and their apologists, but by those who never gave up on the promise of the Universal Declaration of Human Rights—Wolfgang Kaleck will be one of the primary authors. Until then, we can be grateful that he has chosen to write this account of struggles well fought.

Edward Snowden

May 2018, Moscow

FOREWORD TO THE ENGLISH TRANSLATION

Not everything that is faced can be changed; but nothing
can be changed until it is faced.

James Baldwin

Three years on: 2015–2018

A lot has changed since this book was first published in German in 2015.
The Brexit vote, the election of Trump, the rise of right-wing extrem-
ism and racism: such developments have at times made me question
whether lawyers can remain optimistic about enforcing human rights
by legal means. But after much consideration, I've concluded that the
hope reflected in the narratives making up this book is still justified.
In this foreword are some of my key working experiences over the last
three years. I believe they show that working as a human rights lawyer
today, though immensely challenging, still carries considerable potential for necessary change.

Moscow/Berlin, April 2018

Turbulence. This time around the return flight with Aeroflot to Berlin
is anything but smooth. These flying visits to Moscow, which have
become a constant in my life since January 2014, are characterized
by a tension between hope and despair. The revelations from Edward
Snowden—the man I am representing and whom I visit every few

months in the Russian capital—were a result of extraordinary courage. In June 2013 the then twenty-nine-year-old provided us with evidence and detailed commentary confirming that mass surveillance by intelligence agencies and their technological capacities went far beyond the dystopia depicted in George Orwell's *1984*. By revealing this information he risked his life, or at the very least his freedom.

Snowden's combination of courage and humility and his belief that the world could be changed for the better made him a beacon for millions of young people around the world. But there is no doubt that he had hoped his efforts would bring about more political and legal changes than has been the case until now. For many, the shock at the abuses that were exposed was ultimately greater than any willingness or capacity to address the problem in a serious and sustainable manner. That said, there is certainly evidence that the mass surveillance provided by the Snowden revelations is now firmly fixed in the public consciousness. People think of the time before and after Snowden. For all of us, use of the Internet and social media has forever lost its innocence.

Edward's own life is permeated by an extreme ambivalence. Naturally, he is glad that he has not—as of yet—been forced to serve a long jail sentence, probably in solitary confinement at a maximum security prison. This is what he would face if arrested and extradited to the United States, despite the fact that he is a textbook example of a whistle-blower motivated by conscience and a desire to shed light on unlawful acts. Under the 1914 Espionage Act—a sinister masterpiece of political injustice—he could face a thirty-year prison term for each file he copied and made public, an absurd total sentence of several thousand years. The Special Administrative Measures (SAM), which can be applied to those who shared confidential information, mean he could spend the rest of his life in total isolation.

He appreciates that from Moscow he can, in a variety of ways, warn us about the dangers of state surveillance as well as the activities of big tech companies, especially after the latest revelations about Facebook. As an engineer interested in solutions and solution-oriented action, he is sometimes reluctant to believe that societal problems are not as easy to solve as technical challenges.

Snowden can, more or less, move about freely in Moscow. He is also able, with only a few restrictions, to speak his mind, something he does regularly by video link to meetings and events around the world. At the tenth anniversary of the European Center for Constitutional and Human Rights (ECCHR) in Berlin, a human rights organization I set up—joined by a small, dedicated group of young lawyers—we recently had the chance to witness a live video discussion between Snowden and his US lawyer, Ben Wizner. My heart sank when Edward started criticizing Russian actions against the communications app Telegram, which Russia banned after the company refused to share its encryption keys with the state. I wondered if it was really necessary for him to take on the government of one of the few places in the world where he is safe from the reaches of revenge-minded figures like US president Donald Trump and Secretary of State Mike Pompeo, both of whom have called for him to face the death penalty.

The audience in the Berlin theater responded enthusiastically. Once again I was saddened that Snowden had to speak from Moscow and couldn't be there on stage with us. It doesn't reflect well on the status of civil and human rights in Germany and the rest of Europe that no government here has been courageous enough to offer him safe harbor or at least work with like-minded states to provide a home for him in some other part of the world.

The ten-year anniversary party was memorable for another other reason. It marked the endurance of our own organization and celebrated the fact that all around the world—including in places where indescribable horrors continue to unfold—people continue to fight for the rights of others. We have been able to create links between many of these diverse initiatives.

Such collaborations would have been unthinkable ten or fifteen years ago. Take, for example, our lawsuit against German clothing company KiK at the Regional Court in Dortmund, concerning the firm's joint responsibility for the deaths of 259 people in a fire at a textile factory in Karachi, Pakistan, on September 11, 2012. Survivors and relatives of the victims, working with German lawyers and development workers as well as Pakistani lawyers and trade unions in a struggle for labor rights in Pakistan, attracted support not only from the Pakistani public but also from many in Germany. Will we be successful in building something approaching real international solidarity? Might this political impulse—to date the preserve only of small sections of the Left—become a powerful force? There are signs that we have indeed managed to introduce a kind of globalization-from-below, to initiate and sustain human rights litigation that traverses national borders.

But as Albert Camus wrote, "there is no love of life without despair about life." Our work is always characterized by dramatic ups and downs. How could one not despair to see such an egomaniac as Donald Trump, apparently devoid of any human goodness, become the US president; or the torture apologist Mike Pompeo become secretary of state; or Gina Haspel, someone who was intricately involved in the US torture program, be appointed as CIA director? But, over the past few years, together with US partner organizations like the Center for Constitutional Rights in New York, we have managed to gather solid evidence pointing to the liability of prominent US officials and CIA agents and submit it to prosecutors in Europe. Recently the German Federal Prosecutor's Office, responding to a question in Parliament from the Green Party after Gina Haspel was nominated, said it was carrying out preliminary inquiries into CIA torture and if Haspel were to visit Germany and was not covered by diplomatic immunity, she could face criminal procedural measures. That should go without saying, you might think; of course Gina Haspel should be subject to the law like any other citizen. But it's a clear improvement on the situation a decade and a half ago, when the likes of then-Defense Secretary Donald Rumsfeld saw themselves as untouchable, secure in the belief that nobody would ever challenge them or call for them to be held accountable under law for what they did ostensibly in the name of national security.

My first encounters with the Center for Constitutional Rights, including its former presidents Michael Ratner and Peter Weiss, and our work against US torture—discussed in more depth later in the book—marked the genesis of our European Center for Constitutional and Human Rights in Berlin. It was also the start of one of the most important friendships of my life. I still miss Michael Ratner. In early summer 2015, I discussed this books with him, and we spoke about whether my cautiously optimistic assessments properly reflected our joint political and legal work. He was diagnosed with cancer a short time later and died in May 2016.

Michael worked with me for the last twelve years on the Rumsfeld case and played a crucial role in the establishment of the European Center for Constitutional and Human Rights. His personality, experience, and fighting spirit were crucial in the establishment of our organization. Michael was not one of those egocentric macho leftist lawyers. He was willing to share his experience openly and honestly, never seeking to place himself in the limelight. He was an internationalist with a genuine interest in the causes we fight for and the people with whom we work. He was characterized by what you could call revolutionary patience and modesty, and my colleagues and I were able to learn a lot from him. He was a "one-man force multiplier;" he could mobilize and inspire lawyers of all ages across the United States and in Europe.

That is perhaps the greatest privilege of our work: collaborating with highly impressive partners on some of the most pressing problems facing the world. One such person is Colin Gonsalves, the charismatic leader of India's Human Rights Law Network whom I met in 2008 when we just started with ECCHR's work. He invited a group of us to visit India to study its human rights problems and the resistance to them that was underway. He wanted us to get out from behind our privileged and comfortable desks in law firms and NGO offices in New York, London, and Berlin, to leave behind our paternalistic attitudes and work together to develop a genuinely collaborative transnational legal approach. He was motivated by his experiences with garment workers' trade unions in December 2017. For his human rights work over the past several decades, he was awarded the Right Livelihood Award, the alternative Nobel Prize, in Stockholm. At the award ceremony, he argued that the typical focus in the northern hemisphere and the West on individual political and civil rights is too narrow to challenge the problems currently facing humanity. In Stockholm, he called instead for collective legal action, giving a number of examples of how this has worked in the past, some of which are described later in this book.

Following Colin's invitation, I visited the subcontinent in December 2015 and January 2016. I traveled from the far eastern Andaman Islands—closer to Thailand than to the Indian mainland—to the northeastern states of Assam and Manipur, where emergency and special laws are in force, as well as to Delhi, Nagpur in the state of Maharashtra, and finally to Bombay.

At every stop around the subcontinent, I was shocked to see the enduring impact of British colonialism: the deep divisions in the country, the unequal power relations, the poverty, class and caste antagonism, and a story of violence as a kind of overarching history. I have always considered the United States to be a violent country—involved as it is in wars and military interventions abroad while oppressing black and marginalized people at home. But I didn't connect such violence with India, "the world's biggest democracy," a place many of us still associate with the non-violent and anti-colonial resistance of Mahatma Ghandi. Now, I was struck by the extent of the force that the central government exercises to hold together this vast state of states.

India's history of forcibly evicting indigenous people started in the Andaman Islands when British and other Western settlers progressively eradicated the indigenous populations of the islands as well as their culture. This was followed by a similar postcolonial approach by the central Indian government, which settled people from the mainland on the islands. After that came the travelers and tourists, all contributing to threats to the local way of life and to the destruction of the environment, with the result that even the famous coral reefs, the island's most prized attraction, are on the brink of disappearance.

While the legacy of colonial and postcolonial violence, as well as more contemporary destruction by Indian and foreign corporations, can be felt everywhere, I also found a strong resistance everywhere in the country. My friends Colin and Kranti did not accompany me for the whole trip, instead arranging for me to meet some of their colleagues, teams of young lawyers who are fearlessly fighting corporate exploitation, discrimination, and arbitrary killings by police and military forces. And it is not just the lawyers involved in this ongoing resistance.

Assam, January 2016

We leave Guwahati, the capital city of the state of Assam in northeast India, and drive up along the Brahmaputra Valley toward the tea plantations. Tea is one of the few resources in the extremely poor provinces in the northeast. To get to this area you have to pass through the "chicken's neck," a small corridor between Bangladesh and Nepal linking the region with the rest of India. While all of India comprises a multitude of ethnicities, languages, and cultures, here it is especially noticeable, in part because there are so many conflicts that are characterized as ethnic, though they are often rooted more in social and economic issues. The flames of these conflicts were fanned by Britain's immigration policies and, later, those of India's central government.

For the arduous work in the tea plantations, the British brought in workers from indigenous communities in the Indian states of Bihar, Jharkhand, and Chhattisgarh. We meet with representatives of these workers in the small town of Mazbat in the heart of the tea-growing region. They are students from the Adivasi Students Union, the first of their families to go on to higher education, made possible for them through the sacrifices of their relatives. Throughout the day they stress the importance of the law and access to education. Their work is closely aligned with the needs of their community. They organize demonstrations for higher wages. We drive with them for miles into the plantations, where the tea bushes are currently being trimmed back ahead of the first harvest in three months' time. The workers live in settlements at the edges of the plantations and are dependent on the owners for everything. Some are employed permanently, others only on a temporary basis during the harvest. The wages are paltry for this demanding physical work, around 100 rupees or US$1.50 a day. This is not enough to meet even the most basic needs of a family. No wonder, then, that many children quit school to work and help support their families. The few trade unions that organize are all closely linked with the plantation owners.

To add insult to injury, the loose-leaf tea we buy in the supermarket in Germany costs only marginally more than the poor quality tea dust that is sold in India. Even in Assam the tea comes in tea bags; it's almost impossible to buy loose-leaf tea here. Given these deeply unfair structures, the fair trade movement can help only to a limited extent; the monitoring often falls short, and fair trade products account for only 5 percent of total sales. It is clear that the system itself is the problem.

This is evident too during my trip to Imphal, the capital of Manipur, or "India's Burma," as an English friend of mine described it in a human rights report, a move which saw him subsequently banned from entering India. He was referring to the arbitrary police checks, constant police presence, and hundreds of cases of enforced disappearances and extrajudicial killings over the past decades. When there, we meet a group of relatives of people who were disappeared or killed. Sitting cross-legged on the floor in a wooden house we drink tea and listen to their stories. The women present have overcome an inculcated tendency to simply accept their fate and tell their painful stories in public. They have come together to fight for their rights, and their endeavors have brought about some spectacular successes. The Indian legal system has not completely fallen in line with the repressive practices of the government of Hindu nationalist Narendra Modi. In January 2018, the Indian Supreme Court ruled on a complaint brought by a group we met in Manipur concerning 1,529 cases of killings recorded from 1979 to 2012. The Indian government was ordered to carry out investigations into 87 killings committed by police, military, and paramilitary forces.

The group is like many others assisted by young lawyers from the region. Human Rights Law Network (HRLN) trains these lawyers in Delhi and Bombay before giving them roles with great responsibility in regional offices. What is fascinating for me is how they all clamor to work in the communities they come from and how proud they are to have finished their law studies, in many cases the first people from their marginalized communities to do so.

I see this again, during perhaps the most difficult part of my trip, when I arrive at Dr. Babasaheb Ambedkar International Airport in Nagpur. The airport is named after an important politician representing the Dalit—the caste of the so-called "untouchables." Ambedkar was postcolonial India's first justice minister and the author of the Indian Constitution, which on paper at least is impressive. HRLN's regional office in this city of seven million people is led by the charismatic young Nihal, son of a local Roma family. On his desk in the cramped office sit pictures of Angela Davis and Malcolm X.

As with my other trips to the provinces, a packed program has been prepared for me. But this time it wasn't to be. That evening, on arrival at the hotel, the owner informs me that he has had to spend the whole day at the police station on my account. He has been questioned about me and instructed to inform the police about all my visitors, phone calls, and other movements. Despite this, he says, he isn't annoyed with me. He buys us both a beer and good-naturedly gets his photograph taken with me, the one who has caused him all the trouble. My colleagues book a room close to mine, to be there to help in the event of any nocturnal police visits.

We have to rethink my whole travel program at this point. Not so much because I would be in danger traveling overland to the jungles to visit Roma tribes and indigenous communities, but more because I am now contaminated. I am being watched, and anyone who speaks to me will become a target for police scrutiny if they aren't already. So I spend three days with the lawyers in Nagpur, engaged in countless interesting discussions right up to the final hours of my stay, at which point I begin to feel a bit uneasy. In the hotel lobby, which is full of middle-aged men, one of the lawyers I am with—someone who has already been subject to countless politicized legal actions and frequently forced to defend himself against allegations he belonged to the Maoist guerrilla—signals to me that we are the only civilians in the room. The other thirty to forty people are all plainclothes police and intelligence officers. I am escorted to the airport, glad to be leaving Nagpur and heading for Bombay.

Bombay, the most dazzling metropolis of the subcontinent, exceeds all my expectations. I meet filmmakers, architects, photographers, and slum activists who, at rapid speed, detail the history and politics of the city, and with it of the whole country. Two scenes in particular will stay with me: at the edge of the hypermodern skyscrapers in the city center, picking my way through people lying on the ground outside the countless slums that line the streets, I see a frightened old woman trying to cross the multi-lane highway. Despite her clearly frail condition, she is being honked at and nearly run over by drivers. Later that day I'm sitting in a journalists' club, not especially fancy but still worlds apart from the scenes outside on the streets. I'm leafing through a catalog from the photographer Suharak Olwe, who has spent years with the garbage workers of Bombay, capturing them both at work and at home. Suharak's images show Dalit men and women picking through litter—still the only work they are allowed to do—in poor clothes with no kind of protection, immersed up to their heads in deep holes containing human excrement. In their dwellings, many have hung up portraits of Dr. Ambedkar, still a symbol of the hope that the human rights to which they are entitled can be achieved. I am reminded that the right to have rights is a constant theme in our work.

Berlin and Karlsruhe, May–June 2017

A lesson on torture

I meet someone I will call just Munem H. in a breakfast café at Treptower Park in Berlin. He is a suave man in his mid-fifties, with a stocky build. He is dressed in a suit but is wearing industrial boots that don't at all go with the rest of his outfit. Always bringing a good deal of gallows humor to our conversations, he is typical of many of his colleagues in the Syrian legal profession though he is one of its most prominent members. Seeing us jesting with each other as we walk down the street toward the Berlin branch of the federal German police, you couldn't tell which of us was the client and which the lawyer.

And so it goes for the first two hours of his witness testimony. He engages in lighthearted banter with the police officers, kids around with the translators while holding a cup of coffee in his hand, always maintaining his poise and exuding likeability. We spend a long time discussing biographical details. He comes from a Christian family; his siblings—a cosmetic surgeon and an engineer—live in Canada. He studied in Beirut and Damascus. An educated Arab lawyer with a strong work ethic, he was, until 2015, a well-regarded, if not universally liked, citizen of his country.

After a while, it becomes clear that we are skirting around the main topic of today's witness hearing. It's not hard to understand why. In early 2015 at the Syrian-Lebanese border, Munem, along with his wife and son, were taken from their car and arrested. At first, still in lawyer mode, he asked those making the arrest where they were taking him. He was allowed to pass this message on to his wife. He was then driven forty miles back to Al-Qassaa district in Damascus, to the notorious Branch 235 on the street leading to the airport. It housed the Syrian military intelligence, infamous for its systematic torture.

Munem goes on to relate what then happened to him, a story that is close to unbearable for all of us gathered in the room in Berlin-Treptow. Everything happened very quickly, he says. As soon as he arrived at the prison, he was taken to a basement where he was lined up against the wall with other detainees. They were ordered to strip naked and were searched. From all directions, they could hear the screams of people being tortured. They were forced to stand for several hours with their hands on their backs; detainees needing the toilet were forced to relieve themselves in this standing position. After six or seven hours he passed out. When he regained consciousness, he was in a cell with over eighty others. Everyone had been given a number, which, from that point on, was the name by which they were called. The cell was so small that everybody had to stand, except for a small group of the dying, who lay in one corner. For the first couple of days, they were given nothing to eat or drink. There was no toilet. He lost and regained consciousness repeatedly. There were no doctors to attend to the sick. After a few days, he became infested with lice. He lost all sense of time.

All of this he recounts in a staccato manner. When follow-up questions are posed to him, he laughs, attempting to fend off his fear. He asks himself—and us—how it can be that, after just one or two days, a strong and healthy man like him could suffer an almost total breakdown.

He continues his story: after three days in prison he was called for interrogation and had to be carried there by two men. He was brought to a corridor full of people, some of them lying on the ground. All around people were being tortured. When his turn finally came, he was not even asked his name, no allegations were put to him; that's not what any of this was about. He was made to sit on a stool and was then beaten and electrocuted, mostly on the nipples. Once again he passed out. At this point, he lost any remaining sense of time.

Now, in this room at the police station in Berlin, he begins to cry.

He goes on to tell us how, during his interrogations in branch 235 in Damascus, he was beaten on the head with plastic pipes, something that continued until he could no longer speak. He then lost his sight. The interrogators rammed pens into his body; broken pen nibs lay all around. The floor was soaked with blood. There were no questions; the only aim was to inflict pain. After just a few days he could no longer walk. Neither could he remember anything. He was laid in the corner with the dying, the rats gnawing on their bodies.

The guards then dragged him to another interrogation. He was given a glass of water and a potato. He was administered sugared water by way of a drip. He was left sitting there for several hours. The interrogator told him he should rest. He was then handed his clothes and possessions. "You are now free," they told him. He still could not walk. They brought him out of the prison and left him on the side of the street. It took him around an hour to move from one side of the street to the other. He managed to hail a taxi. His phone, which he had been handed back with rest of his possessions, started to ring. His wife was calling him. He asked the taxi driver to take him to a petrol station in another part of town. He wanted to go to a friend's house to recover for a night so that he could go back home on his own two feet. At his friend's place, he drank tea, washed his face, and put on cologne. The next day he learned how his life had been spared.

What saved him was his presence of mind just after he got arrested. After he insisted on being told exactly where he was being taken and was able to inform his wife, she mobilized the church and the lawyers' association and got some public attention for his plight. Through various means, his supporters put pressure on the authorities. He came to think that he had been dead but managed to come back to life. Now he has to give his testimony. He hopes that justice will be achieved; he has to have this hope. Otherwise, he wouldn't be able to go on.

On several occasions, we have to pause the session in Berlin to give Munem time to recover. But at this stage cigarette breaks and going for fresh air don't help. It becomes impossible to carry out an orderly interview. As quickly as he was brought to the brink of death in prison, so too he goes through a rapid physical transformation in the course of the interview, metamorphosing from a confident, dignified lawyer to the humiliated person his torturers sought to make of him. He tries to fight it, but it isn't easy.

After several hours of interviewing we are all drained. Munem and I go to a Turkish restaurant and talk for a while. He now lives in northern Germany, but his immigrant status makes life difficult. He wants to work but doesn't speak much German. The only thing he has is a poorly paid temporary job in a restaurant. He's not sure he can stick it out. He may have survived prison, but they have almost managed to destroy his very means of existence. It is a lesson about how torture works.

As international criminal justice forums are blocked for Syria, these mechanisms don't have jurisdiction over the conflict. But a number of us from human rights organizations are working in several European countries to bring about investigations, and ultimately prosecutions, of the torturers, especially those in positions of power.

Our most important allies in this fight are the Syrian human rights lawyers living in exile in Germany, especially Anwar al-Bunni and Mazen Darwish, two award-winning lawyers highly regarded in opposition circles. Both were themselves tortured by the regime. A few weeks after the hearing described above I accompany Mazen Darwish to his witness interview at the German federal prosecutor's central office in Karlsruhe. We have dinner in a garden restaurant and meet for breakfast the next morning, all the while discussing Syrian, German, and world politics.

Before we enter the building of the prosecutor's office, he answers some questions from a TV crew that is making a documentary about him and his work. We are warmly received and begin to speak to the police officers and prosecutors leading the interview. Once again it becomes painfully clear that we are all avoiding the real subject. We spend hours poring over maps of Damascus, looking for certain places, filling in the biographical details. Yet we know we are here to discuss something else.

We ask for a break after I notice that Mazen is getting angry and aggressive. We go for a cigarette and he then says what's on his mind. He explains that the interpreter, whom I didn't much like myself, has an arrogant, condescending, and domineering style when talking to Mazen. It brings up memories of his interrogations in Damascus. We consider breaking off the interrogation. But the prosecutor is attentive to the situation and figures out what's going on. He instructs the interpreter to behave in an appropriate manner and we make it to the end of the first day.

On a cigarette break on the second day, Mazen and I talk again and then, when we get back to the interviewing room, everything changes. Suddenly Mazen is transported back to the guise of a detainee. He stands up, throws himself on the ground and reenacts the positions he was forced into by the prison guards in Syria: kneeling with his forehead pressed against the wall, waiting to be collected for further torture sessions. He recounts how a Kalashnikov was pointed at him, and that he was then beaten over and over with a cable tie, a plastic pipe, and a club. He describes the "welcome beatings" on his arrival at the 4th Division, and the warning from the cell veteran that new arrivals would be beaten by other detainees until the next detainees arrived.

He tells us that there were more than one hundred detainees in a cell measuring ten by sixteen feet. He relates the arguments that broke out at night when they were forced to try to sleep head to foot, feet on heads, with everyone on their sides to save space. For those with injuries, every tiny movement was a new agony.

Mazen, too, narrowly escaped death. It took him months to recover from the torture he suffered in jail. It's a paradox, but despite the pain it causes him when he tells this story, I silently wish he would keep talking, hoping that this grueling reenactment of torture in a Damascus prison will at least be worthwhile for him - that he and his fellow Syrian activists might one day see some semblance of justice.

The interviews with Munem and Mazen, as well as dozens of other witness hearings, were part of our efforts to push the German Federal Prosecutor's Office to investigate those most responsible for the systematic torture of tens of thousands of activists in the aftermath of the Syrian uprising in the spring of 2011. Using the principle of universal jurisdiction, prosecutors throughout Western Europe are actively looking into the crimes committed in Syria. But until 2018 most of the criminal procedures in Sweden, Germany, or Austria were directed against low ranking perpetrators who happened to find refuge in Europe. Most of them belonged to armed groups like the Islamic State. When we started work—together with our Syrian partners—we decided to target those at the top of the torture apparatus.

A year later, in early June 2018, we celebrated our first success with this strategy: the German Federal Court of Justice issued an arrest warrant against the head of the Syrian Air Force Intelligence Directorate, the infamous Jamil Hassan, a close advisor of President Assad and outspoken advocate of violence and repression. We regarded the warrant as a milestone, not only for the Syrian people in their fight against the impunity of torturers but also in our effort to use human rights law to hold the most powerful accountable. Human rights experts around the world cited our achievement but some academics suggested the decision was primarily symbolic. In doing so, they underestimated the huge impact that the German decision had on people in Syria. Munem, for instance, described to the German and international media the deep relief that he felt when the German courts made their ruling. Mazen Darwish, president of the Syrian Center for Media and Freedom of Expression, declared it the best news he had heard since being released from detention during which he was tortured. Our Syrian colleagues receive e-mails and calls, including from inside Syria, from torture survivors and family members of disappeared and killed activists who were greatly comforted by the fact that, for the first time, a court had determined that a well-known member of the security apparatus was responsible for crimes against humanity. In Berlin, we are aware that an arrest warrant is just a first step, but we also know how immensely important it has been for our Syrian clients and colleagues.

***

Edward Snowden, CIA torture, India, Syria—in a sense these are all continuations of the stories that follow this book. I've gained more experience since they were first published in German, and have perhaps even mellowed somewhat. But these accounts of torture still deeply affect me. I still believe in something my former client, Ellen Marx—a Berliner Jew who fled to Buenos Aires to escape the Nazis—once said to me: there are things that just have to be done, regardless of whether they are ultimately successful.

While writing this foreword on the fiftieth anniversary of the 1968 movement, I come across something said by the French philosophers Henri Lefebvre and Catherine Régulier. It seems apposite to the problems facing us today: "It should be noted: what has died is not possibility, but the desire for possibility, what has disappeared is not change, but the striving for change, what has been extinguished is not life but the yearning to transform it, what is dead is not history but the desire to make it." I am also struck by the observation of the French historian Ludivine Bantigny when she points out what, in her view, made May 1968 in France so unique: the collective political conversation and the collective political action across all classes.

This is something we work toward today. Through collaborative transnational efforts grounded in a justified optimism, we patiently and defiantly face those things we hope to change.

PROLOGUE: A YEAR IN THE LIFE OF A DIFFERENT SORT OF LAWYER

A surreal trip. I still can't quite get used to it. A flight to the other end of the world, from Berlin to Montevideo, from European winter to Latin American summer. I try to relax, find some peace. But it's hard; I'm exhausted. A long walk in the dunes, the feeling of sand underfoot, a swim in the cold, roiling waters. The air is clear; storm rains fell yesterday. I'm seated on the lawn at a white plastic table in the middle of a large puddle. Around me, frogs croak. Bees, butterflies, black hummingbirds, and goldfinches flitter around a bush with orange blossoms. I take it all in. The sun starts to get stronger, I feel like going back to the beach to unwind and leave behind me all my work, including the work on this text. Still reeling from the year gone by, a year that began for me with one great exclamation mark and ended with another, I start to write. About my travels, my encounters, and my work: working with many others, and with the law, to fight for justice. It was an eventful year for us. Despite the unavoidable setbacks, it was a year that managed to elicit some hope of a new and better world. And I come back and write my book at these places which were so deeply connected with my own history.

The Law Society in the City of London, established in 1823, is a place that commands respect. Chandeliers, columns, and carpets of deep red lend the high-ceilinged ballroom a lofty atmosphere. Phil

Shiner, a solicitor from Birmingham in his late fifties, paces back and forth nervously, skimming every now and then through his papers. For ten years his law firm has led proceedings on behalf of hundreds of Iraqi clients who were tortured by British occupying powers after the invasion in March 2003. Tonight in London we are presenting these cases, which we have just submitted as part of a criminal complaint to the International Criminal Court (ICC) in The Hague. In November 2011 Shiner contacted us in Berlin. Us—that is to say the European Center for Constitutional and Human Rights (ECCHR), which I set up with friends and colleagues in 2007 and have led since then as general secretary. Our main goal is to protect and enforce human rights around the world using legal means. Our methods include initiating prosecutions and filing civil lawsuits and complaints to UN bodies; our work plays out in courtrooms and prosecutors' offices and among the wider public. Phil Shiner had reached an impasse with these cases in his home country, despite winning groundbreaking judgments against the United Kingdom from the European Court of Human Rights in Strasburg in two torture cases. Official investigating commissions had examined deaths in detention, including the case of Baha Mousa, a twenty-six-year-old man who died in September 2003 in Basra, in the British occupied zone in southern Iraq after being beaten and abused by British soldiers. While some of the victims have now received compensation, to date there have been no criminal proceedings against those senior officials responsible from the Ministry of Defense and the upper echelons of the military and intelligence services.

Ongoing impunity enjoyed by those bearing the greatest responsibility for grave crimes: it is exactly these kinds of cases that the International Criminal Court in The Hague was set up to address, and a scenario that we have had to struggle against again and again over the years with colleagues and organizations from all over the world. This is why Phil came to Berlin. We've known each other for quite a while. Ever since the United States and its allies launched sweeping attacks on the human rights of terrorist suspects in the wake of September 11, 2001, we've both been part of a small circle of European lawyers taking legal action against these infringements. In Berlin, we analyze reams of reports on the torture and abuse, often involving sexual violence, committed by British soldiers.

On this evening in London, the audience is made up not just of sympathetic supporters from the local universities and human rights organizations. Some seats are taken by well-dressed, middle-aged gentlemen who are clearly not on our side. They are part of the military and intelligence communities and have shown up tonight, a colleague tells me later, to hear for themselves the accusations we are leveling against them. The tone was set by British Foreign Secretary William Hague, who responded to our complaint by describing the British military as the best in the world. They feel targeted and are nervous. I'm not. There's been some initial positive feedback in the media and in our networks, though it remains to be seen how the case will develop from here. But for the moment I won't let myself be distracted by this question. We've worked hard and we have the facts and the law on our side.

A few weeks later we are gathered with our teams from Berlin and Birmingham at the International Criminal Court, a modern, purpose-built building on the outskirts of The Hague, at a meeting with representatives from the office of the prosecutor. They have studied the several hundred pages of our submission and are now asking detailed questions on the contents. The meeting leaves us with a good feeling. We found the right moment to submit the British torture cases at The Hague. The ICC is at this time subject to a great deal of criticism that it investigates only African suspects like Sudanese president Al Bashir.

We are seeking a systematic approach. As it stands, a double stand-ard is applied in international criminal law. The idea of the Nuremberg war crimes tribunals was to apply the criminal law not as a once-off to the defeated Nazi criminals but to continue to apply it universally, potentially even someday against the Allies who sat in judgment in Nuremberg. This project did not succeed at first. No permanent court was established. After World War II and the signing of the Universal Declaration of Human Rights on December 10, 1948, rights violations were committed by many states, and not just the Russias and Chinas of this world. The Western Allies were never held to account by any national or international court for the war crimes they committed on a massive scale in response to anti-colonial liberation struggles: France in former Indochina and in Algeria, Britain in Kenya, the United States in Vietnam.

To date, only Africans have faced charges before the International Criminal Court and a similar double standard can also be found at national courts. More powerful military and economic actors are cur-rently shielded from the reach of international criminal law. But laws that are not applied equally to all soon lose their claim to validity. Their legitimacy crumbles and the system of international criminal justice as a whole is put at risk.

Unlike other critics, I don't see this problem as a sign that it is futile to even try to apply the law; I look at it as an incentive to challenge the status quo. And we do manage to have at least some success in doing so.

After an unexpectedly short wait, we get good news from The Hague: in early May, the chief prosecutor Fatou Bensouda opens a pre-liminary examination into British torture on the basis of our criminal complaint. A few years before, her predecessor had shut down the pre-liminary proceedings in the matter. The decision to reopen the case is a heartening moment that I mark with friends in Berlin that evening.

Among them is Michael Ratner, longtime president of the Center for Constitutional Rights in New York, whose work inspired us to set up a similar organization in Europe.

Moscow, late January 2014

Let's return for a moment to that winter: on January 26, I take an Aeroflot flight to Moscow Sheremetyevo from Berlin's provincial Schönefeld airport, where echoes of the *Realsozialist* past can still be detected in the commands barked by airport personnel. A taxi brings me through the Moscow winter, high-rise apartment blocks, commuter towns, heavy traffic, neon signs, amusement parks, imposing buildings of all kinds. At a hotel downtown, I join a small group of fellow lawyers headed by Ben Wizner from the American Civil Liberties Union. I've known Ben for a decade; we worked together on the case of Khaled al-Masri, a German who was kidnapped by the CIA and tortured in Afghanistan. Now we've come to Moscow to meet with Edward Snowden.

Ever since Edward Snowden's revelations the previous summer, my colleague Carsten Gericke and I have been making arrangements in Berlin to prepare Snowden's legal representation in Europe. We've had meetings to explore the possibility of an asylum request and to assist him in his appearances as an expert witness in front of state inquiries such as at the German Parliament and international bodies like the Council of Europe and the European parliament. In autumn 2013 we assembled a small team of European lawyers and met in Berlin, but until now nothing has been made public. I haven't met Snowden before and I'm looking forward to our encounter.

We get a taxi to the arranged meeting place. Edward Snowden looks just as slight and young as he seems in the photos. But instead of the nerd I'd expected to find, we meet a friendly, open person who begins by giving each of us a gift of a Matrjoschka, a Russian nesting doll. The conversation is straightforward and to the point. Snowden explains, questions, issues requests and directives, but he also listens, understands, and is open to suggestions. There is a long list of topics for discussion, but we swiftly agree on common positions. I feel well primed for the tasks ahead.

While the discussion runs smoothly, the circumstances are deeply unsettling, themselves an intrinsic part and expression of the problem of surveillance: who is intercepting our conversation, who is tracking us, how secure are my office and my apartment back home? My mobile phone suddenly dies; specialists examine it later in Berlin, but the data cannot be retrieved. A sense of threat hangs in the air.

Taking on this case is quite demanding but means a lot to me. We often rely on whistle-blowers like Snowden and WikiLeaks when gathering evidence of human rights violations. The widespread surveillance of purported and actual enemies is something common to secret services all over the world. We work on many such cases because often it is our colleagues—lawyers and human rights defenders—in the Global South who suffer under constant surveillance and the threat of prison and torture.

As a result of this case, I am the subject of increased focus and face something of a balancing act: in my role as a lawyer I am bound to confidentiality and to represent the interests of my client. This means I sometimes have to hold my tongue, which is difficult for me as I follow the self-referential German discussion. Public perception of the case in Germany is marked by a vague sense of concern for German interests, including the tapping of Angela Merkel's mobile phone by the NSA, instead of looking globally at the problem posed by surveillance and possible global remedies.

But I'm also enjoying the chance to work on behalf of this likable person on such an important issue. While I think it's a mistake to revere Snowden as a hero, he has certainly become a symbol, especially for young people, of the good that one person can do. He has set the thing in motion, now the task falls to us all: we need political action against mass surveillance and to improve the protection of whistle-blowers. I fly to Moscow a few more times. As I get to know Snowden better I start to appreciate the breadth of his intellect; his talents go far beyond technical skills.

Buenos Aires, March 2014

It's nearing the end of summer in Argentina. I've been coming to Buenos Aires every year since 1997, both in my role as a lawyer and to visit friends. In that time some things have come full circle for me. For twenty years the crimes of the Argentine military dictatorship (1976–1983) went unpunished, and for the past fifteen years, we have been challenging this impunity in Germany as well as in Argentina. Recently, we have finally started to see some change. Now the special prosecutor tasked with investigating the dictatorship crimes has invited forty prosecutors from all over Argentina to a workshop, and I've been asked to attend as an outside expert. We meet in a tower block on the Avenida de Mayo in the heart of Buenos Aires, five hundred meters from the baby pink presidential palace where every Thursday since 1977 the Mothers of the Plaza de Mayo in their white headscarves do slow laps of the square, demanding to know the truth about what happened to their disappeared children. Truth and justice.

The very fact that this special prosecutor exists and is actually working on the cases, almost forty years after the events in question, is remarkable. In many other countries, similar crimes were never even investigated, let alone the subject of prosecutions. But over the past few years, courts in Argentina have convicted over five hundred senior military, police, and intelligence officers for their role in these acts. The initial trials focused exclusively on uniformed perpetrators, not on civilian collaborators and not on the agricultural, mining, and industrial companies that profited from and supported the dictatorship.

Now, at last, the prosecutors and judges are starting to investigate industrialists, albeit not always as efficiently as we would wish, and not always consistently. I've been working on this issue since 1999 and sued a transnational corporation for crimes committed in Argentina: in 1976 and 1977 trade unionists from a Mercedes-Benz subsidiary in Argentina were kidnapped and murdered. At the workshop, prosecutors from all over the country discuss how it might be possible to investigate, prove, and bring criminal proceedings on the involvement of corporate actors. I can't think of any other country with such a recent history of grave crimes where similar efforts are underway.

Madrid, May 2014

The recent positive developments in Argentina follow trials in Spain, where since the late 1990s judges and prosecutors have been relatively active in pursuing dictators and torturers—initially from Latin America, later from China and the United States. Their work is based on the principle of universal jurisdiction, which states that in the case of the most grave crimes, a state's legal system can take action to prosecute even if the events occurred in a distant country and neither victim nor perpetrator are nationals of that state. For a long time, Spain held firm on this principle in the face of much political resistance. But the conservative government has changed the law and now prosecutors must limit themselves to cases with some link to Spain. An earlier setback came in 2011, when the intrepid investigating judge Baltasar

Garzón was suspended—officially for breaches of the law during a corruption case but in reality, because he had started to investigate crimes from Spain's Francoist past, thus breaking the silence on this chapter of Spanish history. Now he's organized a conference on universal jurisdiction, which he hopes will trigger resistance against these law reforms.

I take my place beside Garzón onstage at Madrid's Goya Theater. I am happy to be able to speak here. A lot of the things that have shaped my work over the past years can be traced back to Spain. It was here that NGOs, lawyers, and Garzón carried out meticulous investigations against the Argentine and Chilean militaries which lead to Scotland Yard arresting Chile's former dictator Augusto Pinochet in London on October 16, 1998. The arrest kindled a powerful spark for me and many others. Suddenly it was possible to imagine how we as European lawyers could work with affected persons and social movements to take transnational legal actions against human rights violations.

I leave the theater early to travel with Madrid lawyer Gonzalo Boye to Algeciras in southern Spain, one of the places where Europe fortifies its borders against refugees. Boye, in his late forties, was born in Chile and had to serve an eight-year prison sentence for alleged involvement in the kidnapping of an industrialist. He's also spent time in the prison in Huelva; he pointed it out to me as we drove by. The region's swampy lands meant that the detainees at the prison were plagued by insects; during his time there Boye had an allergic reaction and fell critically ill. Boye felt he had been unjustly imprisoned and used his time in jail to study law so that he might later be able to help others in similar situations. A person of great determination and grit.

The port city of Algeciras is close to the British-occupied cliffs at Gibraltar. From here you can see the African continent, and this nearness to Morocco can be sensed all around.

The following morning at dawn we board a ferry to Ceuta, a Spanish-occupied enclave on the other side of the Straits of Gibraltar. At the port, Spanish and European flags billow in the wind. But the reality of Ceuta looks a lot different from how Spain and the European Union—an institution that, two years earlier, had been awarded the 2012 Nobel Prize for Peace—would like to present it.

Our taxi driver Ahmed takes us to the hills of El Príncipe, where we look down over the border posting. Here, on February 6, 2014, the Spanish Guardia Civil shot rubber bullets at dozens of black African migrants who were trying to swim across the straits. At least fifteen of them died. This attack is the reason we are here.

Ahmed picks up on our interest and tells us how he was there in his taxi that morning. Hundreds of Moroccans were crossing the border at that time on their way to their precarious jobs as gardeners and domestic workers in Europe. Many of them saw how the uniformed Spanish officers fired, how the defenseless people in the water died, and others were unlawfully brought back over the border. But the Moroccan witnesses were afraid to give evidence. They feared they might lose their visas, threatening their livelihoods. Ahmed has a Spanish passport but still feared police skulduggery.

The criminal proceedings we launched with Spanish human rights organizations against the border guards responsible for the attack are intended to show that the scandalous conditions at the EU's outer borders are a problem for all of Europe. The case is also about enforcing the rights of those who have to date been denied any access to the legal system, enforcing what Hannah Arendt proclaimed as the right to have rights.

Berlin, December 2014

Ceuta is not the only place where people are denied this basic right. In December 2014, the US Senate published its long-awaited report on the CIA's torture of detainees after September 11, 2011. Rumors beforehand indicated that it would document acts of extreme abuse. Republicans and the secret service fought until the last minute to block the publication of this summary report. Now we know why: the protagonists of the Bush Jr. era tortured—and lied. For many observers, what now comes to light was a state apparatus operating beyond any political, judicial, or public oversight: a criminal association fighting to avoid any legal penalties for their many breaches of the law while clamoring to go down in history as the nation's saviors from terrorism.

I've been working on this topic for a decade, so the report contains few surprises. I am, however, heartened to see its global resonance. There's coverage in India and Australia; the *Times*, the *Guardian*, and CNN want to do interviews. It reminds me of events in November 2004 and November 2006, when I worked with the Center for Constitutional Rights in New York to file criminal complaints on the widespread torture of detainees in Iraq and Guantánamo. The complaints were directed against Donald Rumsfeld and former CIA head George Tenet, the latter very much at the center of the latest reports. Our efforts over the last ten years garnered much attention and triggered debate. But for a long time, we had no success with our legal work because prosecutors and other authorities were afraid to go after a country as powerful as the United States of America. That was sometimes difficult for us to accept. But I am certain that the issue would not now be as prominent, and the report would not have been published, if it weren't for our network of people in and outside the United States who over the last several years wrote articles in newspapers and legal journals describing, analyzing, and denouncing these acts.

We also got some tangible results. Former CIA chief lawyer John Rizzo publicly declared that hundreds of CIA agents and their superiors are avoiding traveling to Europe on the advice of their lawyers. They are afraid of being called for questioning or even arrested by one of the prosecution bodies or courts investigating CIA rendition.

The CIA-directed torture is the subject of much heated debate in the United States, but even after the report's publication, there is no prospect of domestic criminal or civil proceedings against the perpetrators and architects of this system. This is the political line held by President Obama since he took office in January 2009. So once again the work falls to us here in Europe. A few days after the news of the report first emerges, we lodge a criminal complaint with German prosecutors in Karlsruhe in a renewed effort to pursue powerful torture perpetrators from the United States.

This kind of work in international networks, the encounters with people and the extensive travel, all started to become second nature to me. I became part of a resistance movement that began in the nineties. It started with improving the law on the books. Building on the legacy of the Nuremberg Trials, grave crimes such as war crimes and crimes against humanity were outlawed. In time it became possible to undertake transnational prosecutions for such crimes. UN tribunals on the genocides in the former Yugoslavia and Rwanda were put in place, followed by the establishment of the International Criminal Court. Lawyers, survivors of political violence, and social movements began to make use of these new legal tools in the face of much resistance. After Pinochet's arrest in the late nineties, it became clear that we as lawyers could take legal steps in Madrid, London, or Berlin to address human rights violations committed abroad but whose root causes often led back to Europe and North America. Over the years these early efforts grew into serious interventions; from individual actions arose a systematic collaboration by actors in various parts of the world. I want to describe these developments, as someone who initially witnessed, criticized and grew indignant, before finally finding my calling in mounting legal challenges. I am lucky to have met many impressive people in many different places during this time. It is from their experiences that I have profited and it is their struggles that I seek to support.

So how did it all begin for me?

For though I was only at the beginning of my journey it had become obvious to me that we were at home nowhere but in our partisanship. . . . We tied what was happening in Germany to the events in France, in Spain, in China, and whenever I thought of people in places whose addresses could no longer be determined, had been wiped from my memory so that they would not be blurted out under an extorting interrogation, under torture, people in a small circle, planning the future development of their country, then this global net would always settle on their words, what they said was recorded by a whirring, was indissolubly hitched to what was being blueprinted and carried out in Africa, in Asia and on the American continents. We were individually scattered and simultaneously embraced in a totality, our mission was to make ourselves as conscious as possible of whatever was happening around us. . . .

Peter Weiss, *The Aesthetics of Resistance*

THE REFUSENIK

FROM JÜLICH TO BONN AND BERLIN

For a long time, I had no answer to the question as to why I have been politically active from a young age. For me, it has always been a part of my life, ever since I could think. Until a few years ago it would never have occurred to me that this drive might have something to do with my family history.

I grew up in the sixties and seventies in Jülich, a small town in the Rheinland. My family didn't speak much about the past. My mother was born in 1936 into the German-speaking minority in Transylvania, Romania. Whenever my parents would tell us about old times, it would start with cinema trips in the postwar years in Munich, where they had met while working in a hospital on the Heßstraße—my mother as a cook, and my father as a night porter to finance his physics degree. They never spoke of what had happened before this time. When the war ended my maternal grandfather was held in Soviet detention; my grandmother didn't know exactly where. She bribed Romanian officials to let the rest of the family leave the country. In 1950 she fled by train with her daughter—my mother—and my mother's younger siblings to Freilassing in Bavaria. Here she was reunited with her husband, who had lost a leg in the war but had been treated well by the Russians.

My grandfather was the only one who ever spoke about where he came from. Home for him was Transylvania, "my people." His stories were not steeped in the revanchism of some of those driven from their homes, but his homesickness got on the rest of the family's nerves. "You and your Transylvanians," they would say.

In summer 2008 I visited my Uncle Fritz, my mother's brother. He had started out as a factory worker, had worked hard and now owned several houses in a nice neighborhood in Munich. I found him sweeping the street in front of the housing block. As we entered a nearby pub, a whole table of drinkers greeted him. We took another table, and as we clinked glasses with our first beers of the evening he said, "Those are my people—from the Munich Tafel." Every Friday the Tafel, or food bank, gave out meals to the homeless and others in need. He was one of the organizers. I hadn't known.

Fritz and I got to talking about after the war, when he arrived in Germany with my mother and their other siblings. They had been dirt poor; at the store, they always had to ask for credit. My mother, the oldest child, never went shopping because she was too ashamed. I think of my grandfather, who later got a permanent factory job at a Weidenkaff household appliances plant in Milbertshofen in Munich and proudly proclaimed, "I'm a made man," and who would donate part of his wages whenever he read in the paper about the misfortune of others: an earthquake in Peru, a flood in Turkey. My father's family had also been badly affected by the war. In the turmoil of the last months of fighting, his mother had to flee the Red Army and leave what was then Königsberg, now Kaliningrad, with just my father and his brother and sister, getting caught up again and again in the ever-shifting fronts.

As a boy, I often sat talking with my mother in the kitchen, and as my political identity gradually developed, I tried to make it clear to her that the path of acquiring a nice little home and a car was not the one for me. I accused of her of wanting to raise me to join the petit bourgeoisie. Her disarming response: "I want my children to be normal and not to stand out." Even then I sensed that their memories of migration had left a mark on my parents. But I didn't realize until much later that my own development had been influenced by coming from a family whose history, like that of millions of other Europeans, was one of trauma, of fleeing, and of poverty.

I'm grateful to my parents for never blaming these experiences on some abstract calamity, like so many other postwar Germans did. My mother and father always made it clear to us that the Germans had caused the war and murdered a huge number of European Jews. Even as a child I knew that all my male relatives who were old enough had worn the Wehrmacht uniform, and that one of my great uncles was such a horrible Nazi that the family had broken all ties with him. My mother, a longtime Social Democratic voter, volunteered with the Protestant church and with Terre des Hommes. My father helped put up election posters for Willy Brandt, but then the Social Democrats got too right-wing for him, and he moved to the Green Party, and later left the Greens when they backed the wars in Afghanistan and Iraq. Both have passed on to me their empathy and solidarity for those on the margins, and today I realize how much that has to do with what they and their families had to go through.

***

In 2009 I was invited to a conference in Bucharest on the CIA's rendition and torture of terror suspects and European complicity. Romania was one of the states suspected of having harbored a secret CIA prison. Before this, I had never made any effort to visit my mother's birthplace. But now I took the chance to fly to Transylvania before the conference. In Sibiu I strolled through the historical town center, recently renovated thanks to European grants. I went on to Brateiu, once home to my mother and grandparents. Helena, a Romanian friend of the last of our relatives to come to Germany in the nineties, welcomed me to her home with various cakes along with home-cured bacon and home-brewed schnapps. I looked around the village. Horse-drawn carts and dogs made their way down the muddy, unpaved streets; a few houses had mid-range cars parked outside. The place had a peaceful, friendly air; nearly all the houses were colorfully painted. In the cemetery, I visited my great-grandparents' graves, and then I found myself in front of an orange house with a slate-tiled wooden roof—the house where my mother was born. I was greeted by the current owners, a Roma family. The mother, dressed in red tracksuit bottoms, agreed to be in a photo with me but only if the picture would not show her mismatched running shoes. I called my mother, just to make sure I was in the right place. Before I could describe the house, she interrupted, listing off what was in front of me: "Behind the house is a little hill with fruit trees. Where you're standing there's a stream. If you look down the street to the left you see the school and to the right the church."

Shortly after I returned from my Romanian trip, I met my friend Nino Pusija at an exhibition opening in Berlin-Kreuzberg. Nino is a photographer from Sarajevo. When he heard about the trip I'd just been on, he called for schnapps and raised his glass: "In Bosnia, we say you're not complete until you've seen the house your mother was born in."

***

Like so many others who end up in Berlin, I was raised in the provinces. My hometown of Jülich lies in the flatlands near the Dutch border, and the town's biggest employer was a nuclear research center. Both the research center and the proximity to the border lent the town a certain cosmopolitan air, but as a young person the place still swiftly became too small for me. When we were young, the main attractions for us were the easily accessible Dutch and Belgian discos, the pubs in

Aachen, and the Ratinger Hof, an underground bar in Düsseldorf. I was glad to be able to get out of Jülich when I finished school.

In October 1979, after an extended backpacking trip around Greece, it was time for my military service. At first, I didn't formally refuse to do my service, initially in the hope I wouldn't make it through the medical screening and later due to my somewhat immature idea that as a budding left-wing subversive it might be useful for me to learn how to use a weapon. I turned up to my unit rather defiantly with my long hair and my anti-nuclear power stickers, and over the next two months proceeded to learn a lot about hierarchical, authoritarian structures. The officers treated me quite reasonably—even when after a week I gave up on the plan (never really meant seriously) to learn how to shoot. I rejected the weapon I was assigned and lodged my official refusal to serve. After this I still had to stay on for two months, waiting for the administration to carry out my "examination of conscience," and in the meantime I was on the lookout for confrontation: when officers wanted to teach us about international humanitarian law and I felt this was an attempt to whitewash the civilian cost of war and warmongering in general. I demanded to know what value these rules had when even our allies could commit war crimes with impunity—the French in Algeria and the United States in Vietnam. I wouldn't let up, and in the end, the class had to be brought to an early close. We were made to fill out a long questionnaire for a background check and our superior informed us that the quicker we were finished, the quicker we could finish up for the day. I started asking why they needed so much information about our membership in political parties, our political ideas, and any trips we had made to the Eastern Bloc. I had the general support of the other hundred soldiers in the room, but the beer was waiting for us in the canteen. The longer I carried on the discussion, the more restless the others became, and the more I sensed the might of this system that kept the whole group there waiting and thus left me at the mercy of my peers. And so eventually I stopped asking questions. During this time I not only got firsthand experience of the power and workings of a bureaucracy, but I also learned how to assert myself—something that came in useful later when I left the military to undertake community service.

I was able to make this switch after presenting myself to the military personnel office in Jülich and enduring hours of absurd questioning about my conscience by a bureaucrat from the military and his two bored associates. The interview continued until, to their obvious annoyance, they ran out of objections to my refusal to pick up a weapon in military service. I began my community service with an Order of Malta care service in Cologne. My boss there had previously honed his authoritarian skills as an officer in the army and as a shift supervisor at Ford. He heeded the calls from the politicians, including the now much-lauded former minister Heiner Geißler, and tried to make community service as unpleasant as possible to discourage others who might be tempted to refuse military service. After our shifts, we'd be ordered to drive around the yard in the disability-adapted taxi or to wash the cars, even if they were clean. I managed to switch areas and worked as a carer for mentally ill and severely disabled people in their homes. But the social services in Cologne also proved to be, above all, a bureaucratic apparatus—a surprise to me in a place where the welfare of the individual was supposed to come first. When I started there I was handed a few index cards bearing the names and addresses of the people I was to care for, including a woman with multiple sclerosis, an old man who was distraught after the death of his long-term partner, and a man in his late forties who had dropped out of his army pilot schooling. Working with no professional training, no real induction, and no supervision was a challenge for me, and for them. None of us were prepared for the situation we found ourselves in. The two men were deeply disappointed when my service came to an end. They hadn't realized that I was assigned to them only for a limited time; they wanted a friend, had treated me as such, and refused to accept a replacement after I left.

A group of us doing our community service in Cologne joined forces and started discussing military service, both with and without a weapon. When our supervisors started looking for more detailed reports of our work hours and tasks, we decided to go on strike. We could see that they wanted to make supervision easier and more strictly regiment the system, at the expense of the contact and communication parts of our work that was so valued by the people we looked after. Strikes among community service workers were forbidden—like soldiers, we were under a chain of command—and we soon faced disciplinary measures. Some of us were even transferred to Bavaria. We dodged more serious consequences by getting sick notes to skip work and filling out forms wrong as a form of sabotage. But the feeling of having caved in to the threats left a bitter aftertaste.

***

These experiences were part of the reason I decided to study law. Despite all the obstacles, I had enjoyed working directly with people, but I didn't want to be subjected to authoritarian rules and the dictates of economic efficiency. I hoped that a law degree would allow me to master and apply the existing rules in a way that would help people who suffered under them, while at the same time pursuing political efforts to change or abolish laws where necessary. For many people this represents a problematic contradiction; for me—even now—it does not.

My decision to go to study in Bonn didn't make life easy for me: the city was conservative, and the field of law studies proved to be a bastion of the Right. At the law faculty, nothing was questioned. There was never any mention of the relationship between the existing law and a broader ideal of justice. From day one it was made very clear to us that our job was to apply the existing laws exactly as conveyed to us by our professors—professors who earned tidy sums of money on the side by drafting legal opinions for the nuclear industry or the Christian Democratic government. Most of the textbooks we used were firmly grounded in authoritarian—if not National Socialist—traditions. The more critical law students in the class objected to this, and the debate on the continuity in Germany between the Kaiserreich, National Socialism, and the postwar West German republic became one of the focal points of our politics.

Only a few of the classes on our official curriculum were of interest to me. Bernhard Schlink was the only professor who encouraged me. While attending his fascinating seminar on the German jurist Carl Schmitt, I started to do in-depth study on this theoretician of the counterrevolution and "crown jurist of the Third Reich." His epigones wielded great influence over constitutional and state theory in West Germany, and many elements of Schmitt's theory of the authoritarian state resurfaced in the constitutional law of the state. I wanted to specialize in criminal law though, to defend those who fight for a fair society, as well as those who are marginalized and persecuted by a repressive and disciplinarian state. I wanted to help these people by making use of the protective forms of constitutional and criminal procedural law.

Those of us who took a critical view of the law banded together— we had to in the often hostile environment in Bonn, with its fraternities and student politicians like Guido Westerwelle, who would later become foreign minister and whose right-wing liberal politics were clear even then. We helped each other prepare for exams, debated leftist social criticism, and organized seminars and workshops. With students from other disciplines, we set up a Kritische Universität outside the university itself. We felt the sweeping societal vision of the 1968 generation had failed, but adopted their theoretical inspirations, based on Marx, Luxemburg, Gramsci, Horkheimer, and Adorno. Having studied the Spanish Civil War in great depth, I felt immune from any authoritarian left-wing inclinations. I was greatly influenced by authors from the Weimar Republic—Ernst Toller and Oskar Maria Graf with their autobiographical works *Eine Jugend in Deutschland* and *Wir sind Gefangene*, and the writing of Kurt Tucholsky. They were unique figures, seemingly lost in a time of great turmoil, and through writing found their own position: left-wing, radical, open, independent, and casting a critical eye on everything they saw. For them, the German Communist Party, subordinate to the Comintern, was just as unappealing as the Social Democrats, who tended toward compromise and pacts with the Right in the early days of the Weimar Republic and shortly before its demise, before Hitler took power. The only remaining position for them was as a non-dogmatic leftist somewhere in between them all, a position I always saw as my own as well.

***

The eighties were marked by a mood of great political upheaval. I believed in the potential of political change, just like the hundreds of thousands of people who became politically active across West Germany, not just in Berlin and Hamburg. An alternative scene started to grow across the country in squats and cultural centers, pubs and shops, accompanied by an alternative media. As a kind of counterpoint to the closed theoretical plans of the '68 generation, there emerged a strong culture of single-issue protest, from local disputes on affordable housing to the fight against nuclear power and the peace movement, whose broad supporter base was evident at the big Bonn demonstrations in autumn 1981 and spring 1982. These campaigns were very disparate. Some of these activist groups later found a home in the Green Party, but like many others, I continued with my efforts outside of parliament halls.

The census boycott campaign of 1983 was a powerful experience for me. The work took me somewhere new every day; it was finally time for our legal knowledge to find some practical application. The planned survey of the entire population of the state was against the law, as confirmed a few months later by the Constitutional Court. I was part of a small group of lawyers who pointed this out in brochures and at innumerable public events, warning of the dangers of the surveillance state. We could never have foreseen the scope of the monitoring that would be made possible by technical advances three decades later, to an extent that would make our Orwellian visions seem harmless in comparison. Our group of young lawyers issued an explicit call for a boycott of the census, and also gave legal advice on how individuals could refuse to take part while avoiding any serious consequences. Our aim was to take the fear away from civil disobedience. Still a student at this time, I would spend one day on podiums with members of Parliament and secretaries of state, the next days out at protests and spraying slogans on walls. I became drawn to this mixture of legal and political action, inherent and more fundamental criticisms, as well as the chance to use legal arguments for social mobilization.

I was also involved in the anti-war movement, which helped broaden my horizons to include global events. But like many internationalists from the left-wing solidarity movement, I saw the peace movement and the disarmament campaign in central Europe as apolitical and overly focused on the defense of a supposedly peaceful status quo in Germany. There were many parts of the world afflicted by armed conflict or brutal regimes, and many of them were supported and fueled by the West. We would chant, "*Deutsche Waffen, deutsches Geld morden mit in aller Welt*" (roughly: "German weapons and money help murder around the world").

In 1983 when the peace movement called for a sit-in protest at the Defense Ministry in Bonn against a NATO decision to upgrade its weapons, we demonstrated arm-in-arm in front of the Ministry for Economic Cooperation, highlighting Germany's complicity in the unjust global economy. Afterward, as we headed down the Adenauerallee toward the center of Bonn, I witnessed an extraordinary event in the Juridicum, Bonn University's law and economics building: to avoid the police, the protest march went straight through the building. In my (often deceptive) memory I was, of course, one of the instigators.

During this time I also studied political science, wrote papers on development policy, and took part in protests with the Latin America solidarity movement. We demonstrated against the G7 summit in Bonn in 1985, against the US interventions in Central America, showed our solidarity with Nicaragua. Even then I saw myself as an internationalist, though Latin America was just one of the topics I was interested in. Little did I know that this political theme would soon come to play such a significant role in my life.

SOLIDARITY FROM THE SIDELINES

MEXICO AND GUATEMALA, 1990

After taking the state exams in Bonn I moved to Berlin with my girlfriend, Adele, and started my traineeship at a civil court in Charlottenburg. Adele soon took off to Mexico City for an art project, a snapshot of the growing women's movement there. That is how, in summer 1989, I ended up in this metropolis, what the Aztecs knew as Tenochtitlan. Mexican society was in a state of transformation following the devastating 1985 earthquake; new initiatives and groups had emerged all across the country. I got to know a country with a rich cultural history and rife with social contrasts. We visited the cities of the indigenous, taking the train to Oaxaca, to Palenque in the jungles of Chiapas, and the monumental temples of Chitzen Itza in Yucatan.

I got back from Mexico just as the political upheaval was beginning in East Germany. Germany swiftly pushed for reunification; the opportunity for real change was lost. I was moved and frustrated by the changes. I then decided to return to Mexico to save my relationship. Luckily my friends from the Latin America Information Center in Bonn were able to find a position for me at a Guatemalan human rights organization working in exile in Mexico City, where I spent three months of my legal traineeship.

***

It's autumn of 1990. The *Comisión de Derechos Humanos de Guatemala* has its offices in a small, white two-story house in the middle-class district of Colonia Narvarte. The staff there is very welcoming to me, the organization's only non-Guatemalan. Once a week we gather at a party or in one of the city's many cantinas. Everyone gets increasingly melancholic as the alcohol consumption rises, especially when Fredi gets out his guitar and starts singing. Fredi, mid-twenties, small, stocky, bow-legged, laughs a lot—not a loud or raucous laugh, rather more cautious. He quickly becomes my best friend at the commission. At lunchtime, I pick him up from his corner room upstairs and we go to the nearby market. We eat *comida corrida*, a simple daily specials menu, or a spicy fish soup, followed by a salad made of dozens of kinds of fruits or a Licuado, a fruit shake with water or milk. With my flatmates, two politics professors, I listen to Mexican music for hours on end, especially Augustin Lara, the chansonnier of the golden age between 1930 and 1960, whose boleros are still played all the time: in the cantinas, in the clubs, sometimes in the original, sometimes covered by followers like Tona La Negra, sometimes even by the punk bands who play at a place near our apartment called Look, Mexico's only punk club at the time.

When I arrived in Mexico, Guatemala had been suffering for thirty-five years under more or less openly military rule. In the early eighties, the dictators Lucas García and Ríos Montt pursued a US-backed counter-insurgency policy of scorched earth tactics to rupture civilian support for the leftist guerrillas who'd been fighting the state for decades. The consequences were devastating. In a few years, more than a hundred thousand people were murdered. Around a million more, mostly from the indigenous populations, were forced to flee, and more than four hundred villages were razed to the ground.

As I write this, I'm debating with myself as to whether I should set out these horrors in detail. It might help to make a lot of things clearer, but then the portrayal and the observation of the suffering of others brings its own conflicts. In her essay on photography, Susan Sontag asks the important question, "what to do with the feelings that have been aroused, the knowledge that has been communicated"—do they not lead to boredom, cynicism, and apathy? I also see a danger that we—those of us who work on these issues—only inflate our own importance with dramatic portrayals, as though our own significance rises with the scale of the horrors we report. Aren't we then appropriating the stories from those who have suffered in order to further our own work, even if that work has the best intentions? I choose to follow Sontag's suggestion and reflect on "how our privileges are located on the same map as their suffering, and may ... be linked to their suffering, as the wealth of some may imply the destitution of others ..." Politically it would be wrong to look at the question of human rights violations from a Western, paternalistic point of view, isolated from their political and economic causes in the global capitalist system.

All my colleagues at the commission were forced to flee Guatemala. The longer I work with them, the more I learn about their past. I hear stories about how their education, careers, and entire lives were upended due to the threat posed by the military. On November 1, 1990, we celebrate *Día de los Muertos*, the Day of the Dead. Like millions of people in Mexico and across Central America, my colleagues set up an *ofrenda*, a kind of altar with pictures of the dead and colorful offerings like flowers, wreaths, ribbons, and figurines. Many of the faces in the photos are very young, and each picture tells a story of violence and pain, of torture and murder, of relatives, comrades, or colleagues.

The commission is part of Mexico City's lively Guatemalan exile scene, which at that time also includes Rigoberta Menchú, who would later go on to win the Nobel Peace Prize. A woman who exuded joie de vivre, we would meet her at the exile community's music- and rum-filled events and parties. Rigoberta's family history represents the brutality of the repression suffered by Guatemala's indigenous population. Her parents had taken part in the occupation of the Spanish embassy in Guatemala City, through which demonstrators successfully sought to draw attention to the violent repression. On January 31, 1980, the regime launched airstrikes on the building. Thirty-eight protestors and embassy staff died.

At the commission, our work consists of compiling and publishing reports on recent human rights violations in Guatemala. It's too dangerous for the staff to visit Guatemala and do research there. As a result, the work is fairly monotonous. We sit at our desks in tiny rooms with one or two colleagues, analyze media reports, especially from newspapers, and update lists: the tortured, disappeared, arrested, and murdered. Day after day. There is no police force, no court, and no prosecutor in Guatemala or anywhere else where the victims or our commission could lodge a complaint against the military's crimes.

The work here gives me a dramatic insight into the cycle of exploitation, lawlessness, and resistance, of state repression and impunity. The indigenous population provided a particularly strong example of initially peaceful resistance against the exploitation they faced, exploitation firmly rooted in the country's colonial past. Popular president Jacobo Árbenz took power following democratic elections in 1951. Just four years later he was toppled in a US government–backed putsch, in a move that destroyed any budding sense of democratic participation and resulted in the emergence of a guerrilla movement. Repression by the ruling elite intensified with the civilian population now extensively targeted. Outside Guatemala, the crimes were justified as a necessary evil in the fight against communism and went unchallenged.

I start to understand that the concept of impunity encompasses a complex societal situation that goes far beyond the mere absence of punishment. At this time I take a critical view of German criminal law. I see it as tool of dominion and control, albeit in a more subtle one than in Guatemala, a tool that distracts attention from the social root causes of violence, punishes only certain social deviances, and is thus ill-suited to solving conflicts in society. It's a position I will revisit in the coming years when faced with radical right-wing violence and almost total lawlessness in East Germany. Through my work in Mexico, I'm confronted with a situation in which the state breaks the very promise on which its legitimacy is based, namely that it will protect its citizens. When crimes like mass murder in Guatemala go unpunished, there emerges a culture of violence that is exercised by state and non-state actors and is never challenged. In this social climate, the powerful freely abuse their position to further their own interests; for the rest of the country, exercising fundamental civil rights becomes a risk.

By documenting human rights violations, our aim is to spread the message to an international audience and thus support progressive movements. But nobody is under any illusions at the commission. The former dictator and mass murderer Ríos Montt and his henchmen continue to shape Guatemalan politics, even in times of formal democracy. There are no international courts in existence in 1990. None of us considers that one of the generals might one day be brought before a Guatemalan court. And yet that is exactly what happens. Years later, in May 2013, Ríos Montt is sentenced by a court in Guatemala City to eighty years in prison for genocide—a historical event for local human rights organizations as well as for international criminal law.

During my time in Mexico, I do not foresee how closely involved I will one day be in the fight for such changes. But I do gain a real appreciation of subjects I had previously known only from newspapers and human rights reports; torture and forced displacement become real to me. I understand that crimes of this kind are not mere accidents, not simply the excesses of sadists. They are systematically planned and directly linked to tangible interests: land, raw materials and crops, and the preservation of a centuries-old order under which one side are slaves, the other masters. I get firsthand experience of a class struggle waged from above with all available means, and these impressions, some perhaps merely imagined, leave me forever changed. There is no going back.

***

In my third week, the head of the commission, Anantonia Reyes, a spry, spirited woman in her early thirties, comes to me with an idea. Since 1988, around fifty thousand indigenous women who lost their husbands to the state repression have joined forces under a national association called the Conavigua. These women face discrimination of various kinds, as part of the rural class, because of their ethnic background, as women, and as widows. Anantonia suggests that I write a report on this young organization and travel to Guatemala to witness the celebrations around the two-year anniversary of its establishment. As a German it will be safe for me to do the research, she says.

We start making inquiries in Guatemala. It dawns on me that I'm secretly hoping it won't work out. I'm overwhelmed by the prospect of this trip. My Spanish is only passable, and I'm glad to have somewhat settled into life in Mexico City. In this Moloch of a city, I've found people whom I like and who like me. I've found places I'm fond of, the markets and the cantinas at night, as well as the music.

When I look back now, in early 2015, at my old notes and reflect a bit, I still relate to the young law student I was back then: angry, romantic, indignant, ever questioning. But when I read the entries on my

Guatemala trip, I also see how inexperienced I was at dealing with people from other cultures. The notes point to an inner conflict: I was on the sidelines, a mere observer, but wanted to be more than that; I was aware of my privileged situation and grappling with the distance between me and the struggle of those with whom I declared solidarity. My notes from this time are largely about me and this situation that was so alien to me. It wasn't until later in life that I managed to stop conceiving of these encounters as journeys of political self-discovery and developed real empathy for people affected by injustices. In Germany, there were few people outside the Latin America solidarity movement who were openly describing and criticizing the crimes being committed there and the complicity of the West. And so my work was certainly worthwhile, but at the time there wasn't anything more I could contribute. I did not yet have the requisite access to the legal community, to power, resources, or an audience. Nonetheless, it was a start, and it spurred me on.

***

When the morning of my departure comes around in autumn 1990, I would rather be anywhere but on my way to Guatemala. It's not so much fear that something might happen to me as a vague sense of uneasiness.

From the air, I look down on mountain slopes of deep green and long valleys: what seems like unspoiled nature. As the plane lands at Aurora Airport in Guatemala City, I see the military's olive green planes and helicopters that have brought such widespread death to so many villages that they crop up in countless drawings by children in refugee camps. When I enter the airport, I'm on the lookout for armed soldiers and stocky men with suspicious bulges in their suit jackets, but the dictatorship presents itself to visitors in a friendly, civil fashion.

For the military, the time spent keeping a low profile paid off. Following the 1985 elections, which saw civilian and Christian Democrat Vinicio Cerezo take office as president, international money flowed into the country. Western states, including West Germany, supported the government by providing the police with training and technical equipment, despite the fact that they continued to spy on, arrest, and torture oppositionists. German diplomats helped to bolster the government instead of supporting people from the social movements who were at great risk. In the German embassy, the walls are papered not with calls to support the widows' association but instead with the wanted posters used by the Guatemalan police to criminalize student groups. Human rights are simply not on the German diplomatic agenda at this time. Diplomatic work was seen primarily as a form of overseas trade mission on behalf of Germany and the many Germans and people of German origin in Guatemala, including those involved in plantations who collaborated with the military to eliminate trade unionists.

A taxi takes me from the airport to the Zona Uno, in the heart of this city of two million people. Its busy one-way roads are lined with advertisements, neon lights, and bunting. I feel alone, strolling up and down the narrow streets. Every five minutes I am engulfed in black smoke as one of the decommissioned yellow US school buses thunders past, exhaust pipe fuming. It's the rainy season, and soon it's pouring down, bleak. Some pedestrians look for shelter in doorways and under shop canopies, others hurry along, keeping close to nearby buildings in an attempt to stay dry. The streets fill with rivulets and puddles. One man doesn't pay attention and soon gets soaked by a bus swishing past. He smiles tiredly at his own foolishness.

Two days after I land I'm sitting on a bus. Through the window, I can see a group of schoolchildren in uniform filing along the street, led by a teacher on a bike. The horizon above them opens up to a fantastic view of the volcanoes that surround the sprawling city. I'm on my way to the Coca-Cola trade union headquarters in an industrial district, where today there is a celebration planned to mark the second anniversary of the Conavigua.

A group of indigenous women is gathered at a small dusty square in front of a factory building, washing, combing, and braiding their long black hair. Their skirts and shirts, the ribbons braided into their hair, and the fabric wrapped around their heads like wreaths are all specially made in the colors of their ethnic communities. Pieces of wood are piled up at a muddy patch in the square, a huge pot of coffee sits on the fire, tortillas and beans are prepared.

The hall is decorated with huge swathes of tulle, green plastic garlands, colorful rugs, and embroidered quilts; on the walls hang photos of Coca-Cola trade unionists who were killed over the last fifteen years. The women hang apples, grass, and flowers from lines and empty sacks of grass onto the stage. There is traditional dancing and a minute's silence for those who died or disappeared in the fight, and then a theater piece performed by young students. An actor in an olive green shirt with an army cap, sunglasses, and a blond wig speaks to an indigenous woman named Rosa, making lofty promises of a wonderful future. Rosa is played by lanky guy in a black wig and lipstick, with a frilly red dress pulled over his jeans. The women are mightily amused by him. But after the performance it's right back to reality: the theater group hurries out of the hall, sunglasses on—last spring, actors from the Coca-Cola theater group were murdered.

Afterward, I meet some of the Conavigua women from the province of Quiché, north of Guatemala City. We sit on the grass behind the factory and talk until sunset. They usually have just two small meals a day consisting of tortillas, salt, and beans. At harvest time they look for work on the coffee plantations along the coast. We talk about Maria

Mejía, a colleague of theirs who was murdered in March of that year by the military, who claimed she was linked to the guerrilla. Maria Mejía was one of the national leaders of the Conavigua; her murder was directed against the whole organization. The military banned all assemblies in the province, every meeting was denounced as support for the guerrilla, and individual members were personally threatened. Despite all this, the women did not seem at all despondent. Calmly and clearly, they told their stories with the composure of people who understand that their experiences are shared. They are proud of their organization and find it a great help to be able to speak to their *compañeras* and to see the solidarity from other groups.

The next day I travel to Purrujil II with some of the widows and their children. In 1980 and 1981 the army kidnapped and shot many of the men from this village. One hundred seventy widows still live here with their families. As I step off the bus a breathtaking view appears: the vast Lake Atitlán and the volcanoes that surround it. From the roadway, we walk through cornfields down to the long, narrow settlement. In an unadorned church with white walls and a concrete floor, a Mass is being held to honor the Conavigua. I follow the women into the dark interior of the building, blinded as my eyes adjust, and take a seat. They are all dressed in their traditional costumes, thick skirts, colorful blouses, striped headscarves. I sit around cross-legged for a couple of minutes with the others before realizing that it's only women around me. Feeling uncomfortable, I get up and go over to the men who are sitting on wooden benches against the church's long walls. The entrance is open, giving a clear view of the sunlit hills; children and adults are constantly coming and going. The children look at me with disbelief.

Afterward, I stand around in front of the church, where passersby take the chance to size me up. A group of men in Western clothes approach, and one of them starts to interrogate me. He wants to know if I came to the village because of the widows, if I knew their leaders here. I dodge the conversation. Later I sit on the floor of a small, sparse room with fifteen women from the local Conavigua group. They tell me about their day-to-day lives, while the women from the capital city translate from Cakchiquel into Spanish. They produce textiles together, *tejidos*; any tasks that need to be done are divided up between them. Because they don't have their own fair and functional system of business, they are not adequately paid for their hard work. But ever since they became politically active, they have a new conception of their value as women. They go to demonstrations regularly, most recently in the nearest town to protest against the arrest of one of the townspeople. At the end of our conversation, the women thank me for my concern, saying that they are glad that outsiders are taking an interest in them. It's a comforting moment at the end of this trip, during which I often felt very out of place.

On the bus trip back I chat with Fermina Lopez, an impressive woman who only learned Spanish two years before and who, after one year, traveled all over Europe as a representative for the widows. With a laugh, she tells me how amazed she was to see that even in the countryside every house had electricity, a phone, and a TV and that there were no street vendors.

Then I'm back in Guatemala City, and the contrast could not be greater between this place and my impressions of the past two days, the strength of those courageous women and the bright colors of their costumes. A living community has given way to a collection of lost individuals. Pop music comes blasting out of the bars and shops, the smell of piss lingers along dirty streets lined with people hawking nuts, fruit, a handful of onions or tomatoes. Others beg, most of them women with young children. As the restaurants and shops close and the *avenidas* empty, I wander through the grim streets. Prostitutes stand around;

men stream out of cinemas after the last showing of war and karate movies from the United States. People are lying on the footpaths, bedded down on cardboard boxes or newspapers, their few possessions gathered up under their heads as a pillow. Many are drunk. Two doors from my guesthouse I meet a group of twelve- to fifteen-year-olds. Street kids here are subjected to extreme police violence: officers kick children to death or force them to drink the glue that so many of them sniff. In the newspapers I've seen pictures of teenagers who have been tortured to death, photos of teeth smashed in, ears and tongues sliced off, bodies disfigured with wounds. I feel helpless.

Craving a few days of rest, I leave Guatemala City and head to Antigua, a small city surrounded by volcanoes in the highlands with a well-preserved historical center full of baroque buildings and churches—one of the country's tourist hotspots. The cafés are brimming with young people from the United States and Europe. Hardly any of the ones I talk to know what's going on in the country. They have no clue about the situation of the people serving them, the people selling their wares in the picturesque markets. No one takes any interest when the morning paper carries news of the murder of a trade unionist close to the town. Once again I am left feeling foreign, even now, surrounded by people like me.

Germany and the Germans are preoccupied with their own issues at this time. I follow enthusiastically the fall of the wall and the opening up of Berlin, but am repelled by the national frenzy that follows a year later surrounding German reunification. I skip the celebrations in the German embassy in Mexico to mark the official unification on October 3, 1990. A few days after I get back to Mexico I spend a weekend on the Atlantic coast in Veracruz with my friend Fredi, where we have a pleasant encounter with these historical developments. It's a warm night, Veracruz is filled with music, people are dancing in the streets, different rhythms spill out from the cafés and the arcades; it's all there, from the soulful rancheros and boleros of Augustin Lara to Caribbean rhythms. We are sitting with four East German sailors who have anchored here with their container ship. We tell them about our work and describe the human rights situation in Guatemala and the whole region. They are curious, ask lots of questions, and then tell us about their voyages, including arms shipments to Nicaragua. Then they tell us how on the third of October, in the middle of their journey on the high seas, they took down the East German flag and hoisted up the flag of the *Bundesrepublik*: with a strange feeling and yet without great emotion—neither mourning the old nor celebrating the new.

***

Back in Berlin, my report in Guatemala becomes part of a brochure on the Conavigua; it's not a particularly significant contribution. But I had met people who worked at great personal risk for a more just society. The Guatemalan human rights lawyers whom I was privileged to count as colleagues approached their work with dedication; it wouldn't occur to them to give up. Despite the ever-present tensions, they exuded joie de vivre and embodied a kind of collective spirit that I hadn't encountered in Germany. By taking me on board, they made me a part of their struggle and left me a more earnest person as a result.

He went on to explain how each totemic ancestor, while traveling through the country, was thought to have scattered a trail of words and musical notes along the line of his footprints, and how these Dreaming-tracks lay over the land as 'ways' of communication between the most far-flung tribes.

'A song', he said, 'was both map and direction-finder. Providing you knew the song, you could always find your way across country'...

Aboriginals could not believe the country existed until they could see and sing it—just as, in the Dreamtime, the country had not existed until the Ancestors sang it.

Bruce Chatwin, *The Songlines*

THE NOMAD

MONTEVIDEO AND PATAGONIA, 1996

Berlin was a thrilling city in the early nineties. When the wall fell, we ran into the streets and explored East Berlin. Getting to know the activists, the East Berlin nightlife, the ruins, the cellars—I liked the openness of it all. The left-wing law firm in Kreuzberg where I was doing my traineeship gave me plenty of freedom to take on my own clients, and I represented kids from Kreuzberg's gangs as well as prisoners. Some other young lawyers and I set up a prison group and visited people in the various Berlin jails: politically active long-term prisoners in Moabit and Tegel, and the equally politically active women held at the women's prison at Plötzensee for drug crimes. We talked to them about their cases as well as the generally bleak situation for detainees, in particular the disparity between the state's professed aim in imprisoning people—to reintegrate offenders—and the reality of the situation, in which almost all efforts failed due to a lack of resources. We made plans to set up an in-prison legal advice service, but it was opposed by more established lawyers. During this time I noticed once again how much I enjoyed hands-on work with people. Our prison group also discussed fundamental criticisms of the criminal and prison systems, based in part on Michel Foucault's analysis of the modern system of criminal justice and Otto Kirchheimer and Georg Rusche's classic study on social structures and punishment

(*Sozialstruktur und Strafvollzug*). Kirchheimer and Rusche describe the enforcement of sentences as a rational instrument of dominance, aimed primarily at people from the working class who make up the majority of the prison population.

After qualifying in spring 1991, I set up a law practice with my colleagues Dieter Hummel and Volker Ratzmann in the Haus der Demokratie in East Berlin. The building had once belonged to the Socialist Unity Party but around the time of reunification was sold for one D-Mark to groups from the East German "New Forum" civil rights movement. Our practice specialized in political cases. Over the next few years, I got to know the life stories of Stasi victims, accompanied them to the Stasi archives to see their files, and wondered why we leftists in the West hadn't done more to show solidarity with them. I defended people who rejected military service and those who refused to do any kind of alternative civil service. I also defended victims of Neo-Nazi violence, which brought me to many corners of the former East, and gradually I got to know Magdeburg, Halle, Rostock, Leipzig, and Dresden.

My work with the Guatemalan human rights commission was already some time ago, but it had left its mark on me, and I felt connected to the struggles going on there. But by that stage, I still could not have predicted that I would later play a role in the legal efforts to overcome impunity for state crimes in Latin America. In 1996 I traveled to Uruguay, Chile, Brazil, and Argentina. It was a personal trip, but it would turn out to be important for my work in the future as well. I returned not only having seen a magnificent landscape and discovered traces of past political battles, but also with a new sense of feeling at home among these cultures and people.

***

Montevideo is a peaceful city. I arrive there with a friend in December 1996, bleary-eyed after a long transatlantic flight, having swapped the Berlin cold for South American summer. The taxi brings us from the airport to Barrio Sur, a neighborhood where many black people live, the descendants of Brazilian migrants. We stop in front of a lovingly restored old townhouse. It belongs to David Campora, whom I met through friends in Berlin, and his partner. David opens the door, laughs, and hugs us. He is sixty-four years old, with an athletic body tanned from years of sun. "Do you feel like a swim, or breakfast?" he asks. We are just in the door when the doorbell rings and some boys ask if they can do some drumming for the Portuguese guys. The Portuguese—that's us, the name they use to denote all white people that came after the Portuguese colonization of Brazil.

That evening I have my first ever *asado*, a traditional barbeque in Uruguay and other countries in South America. David puts pieces of wood in the metal basket of his big, walled barbeque before lighting them and carefully distributing the glowing embers below. Then the various courses are placed on the grill: the provolone, morcilla (blood sausages filled with nuts), spicy chorizo and salchichón, onions, garlic, leeks, sweet potatoes, bell peppers, corn on the cob, and the pièce de résistance, a large piece of beef. We eat, drink, and talk in a small, lively group. It's a wonderful evening, and as the feast comes to an end, we listen to music spilling over from the streets. The doorbell rings: it's them again, the four boys with the Candomblé drums. This time we ask them in, and they start playing wildly, with the virtuosity of those who have grown up surrounded by music.

David Campora was one the heads of the Tupamaros, Uruguay's urban guerrilla, which came to the world's attention for its Robin Hood-style redistribution actions as well as for the murder of US citizen Dan Mitrione, one of the instructors sent to teach Latin American torturers.

Over the next few days, we talk a lot about Uruguay, a state ruled by the military from 1974 to 1985, and about the history of leftist movements. Like so many leftist utopias, theirs failed due to their own miscalculations and the superior might of the old elite. David spent eight years imprisoned in the junta's jails and barracks where, like all the political prisoners, he was tortured. He endured eight years of daily indignities and the constant fear of imminent death. In some ways, he was also lucky. His wife and three children managed to flee to Germany through Chile and start a solidarity campaign for him that eventually led to his release, allowing him to join them in Germany.

He returned home soon after the military lost power in 1985 and was elected an executive committee member of the Tupamaros, who had by then formed a political party. Campora, a financial auditor by training who relishes research, got to work analyzing the papers obtained through the guerrilla on economic corruption and confessions of the death squad members captured by the guerrilla, as well as the CIA handbook that served as a torture manual for the Uruguayan and many other Latin American militaries. Today he works on the archive of the guerrilla, hoping to shed light on the political failure of that time. A friend of his often makes fun of him: "You're only happy when you can neatly file reality away in folders." With a laugh, he counters: "Give me a folder that's big enough, and I'll file all of reality away in it for you." He is looking into events like the 1971 murder by the guerrilla of a farmer who had accidentally stumbled upon one of their weapons depots, in David's view an unforgivable act for a movement that never wanted to be elitist, that saw itself as close to the people. The murder of torturers and death squad members on April 14, 1972, before the beginning of the dictatorship—that ultimately led to David's arrest—was in his view another grave error on the part of an already ailing grouping. At the same time, the heroic history of the organization is what gives it its political capital. The group is part of the Frente Amplio, the large leftist coalition, and at the time of my visit is aiming to make political gains.

What's interesting for me is the clarity with which David analyzes the history of his movement and insists that it should be held up to scrutiny. Despite his firsthand and painful experiences following the political defeat, he has not given up, and he is not one of those frustrated old men who live only in the past. He feels a strong connection with the Frente Amplio project and knows all the protagonists but has still managed to maintain a critical distance from them, without losing his hope. For him it's about the truth, that's what he wants to document. I find his approach to the—at least preliminary—failure of a political project impressive in part because it would be unimaginable in the German Left.

After a few days, I say farewell to David and begin the part of my trip I'd been most looking forward to since another had gone before me and written about his travels. Bruce Chatwin's stories about Patagonia and its people had left a strong impression on me; in them, I'd heard echoes of my own disquiet. Chatwin says that humans are born to be nomads, an idea that aligned with my own feeling and reinforced my own love of travel. When in motion I feel a sense of belonging. On the road, I am the person I want to be and want to become. With Chatwin at my side, I don't feel like an outsider, someone who just failed to find a place to call home.

Argentina has a rich history of immigration, and you can still sense that there today. In the late nineteenth and early twentieth centuries several waves of Europeans arrived, mostly Spaniards and Italians, many of them organized in socialist and anarchist groups. Today only a small proportion of Argentineans are descendant from the indigenous peoples almost entirely wiped out in colonial times by the Spanish and, in the nineteenth century, by the Argentine Army. Reading the

German-Argentine writer Osvaldo Bayer, I learned about Rebellious
Patagonia and the brutal class wars of the 1920s. Bruce Chatwin also
writes about the events of this time. The agricultural workers from
Chile and southern Europe fought desperately for better working conditions and against repression by an army determined to preserve the
quasi-feudal status quo and the dominance of the Estancieros, the big
landowners, and who viciously defended the meat industry capitalists.

By chance, I find the Estancia Anita. I'm sitting in a tourist bus
heading through Patagonia, this vast, coarse stretch of land that spans
the southernmost tips of Chile and Argentina. The young tour guide is
describing the rest of our route from the provincial capital El Calafate
to the Perito Moreno glacier and happens to mention that we are currently passing the Estancia La Anita. La Anita? That rings a bell, I think
to myself, and then I remember that Chatwin had written about this
place, a ranch on which a group of strikers were massacred by the military during the big farm worker strikes of 1921 and 1922. "Why," I
ask our guide in front of the group, "don't you mention this part of the
story?" He makes some excuses, and I tell what I know to the woman
from Buenos Aires sitting beside me who is curious about the story.
Later on, our guide sits next to me and explains, "Of course I know
about the massacre, everyone here knows about it, but the powerful
families around here don't want people to talk about it. I'm a student.
I need the income from this job." I'm drawn to Puerto Natales in Chile
for the same reason as so many other travelers: its proximity to the
Punta Arenas port and the Torres del Paine National Park. I've booked a
four-day trip on a repurposed cargo ship through the southern Chilean
fjords through to Puerto Montt in the north. But the bad weather delays
our ship. Stranded for a while, I eat lamb and drink beer. In a stationery
shop, I find a cabinet with local histories. Browsing through the books,
I find a story that unfolded here in Puerto Natales in 1919. In January

of that year workers at a cooling plant went on strike to fight for the eight-hour day and then overran the local gendarme, taking control of the area until the Argentine and Chilean militaries joined with police forces to end the uprising. Several workers were shot and twenty-seven others arrested. In the old graveyard, I easily spot the freshly painted green and white monument for the police. I have to look a lot longer to find the graves of the workers and communards who were shot. I finally find them, totally neglected at the edge of the graveyard, and stay awhile in silent thought.

Why do I bother with these stories from long ago? I've always seen myself as part of a universal leftist history, connected to the struggles, the triumphs, and the defeats of the past. I think what drives me is the question of why people take a stand in some historical moments but don't in others, and what we could learn from this.

The commune of Puerto Natales lasted just a couple of days before the old order was restored. A taxi driver takes me the seven kilometers to Puerto Bories, to the spot where the clashes took place. One of the old refrigeration buildings is now a chic hotel, the meat factory has long been closed down, the whole site is fenced off, entry forbidden. On the side facing the beach, the fence has been trampled down. I take a look around. A few people sit on the old jetty fishing for salmon. One woman has 1950s rock and roll blaring from her transistor radio. Nobody is able to tell me about the history of the place. There is no indication that this was once one of the biggest meat processing plants in the country, and there are no memorials to the dramatic events that played out here nearly ninety years ago. Beyond the fjord, the snow-covered mountains and the Balmaceda glacier glisten in the distance.

At the start of his travel diary, Chatwin writes that never in his life has he wanted anything as he wanted this one piece of skin. He was referring to a piece of leathery skin from a mylodon—a now extinct kind of giant sloth—that he had found as a child at his grandmother's house in England after a cousin had sent it back to her. When his grandmother died, he said to his mother, "Now can I have the piece of brontosaurus?" She answered, "Oh, that thing! I'm afraid we threw it away." I take a taxi from Puerto Natales and head toward the Cerro Benitez Mountain. There's a large cave here with a fantastic view, and it's said that a mylodon once lived here. I get there and, of course, find nothing.

I want to know what it looks like on the estancias, the vast cattle farms described by Chatwin, want to understand what life is like here, and so I travel on toward the Rio Grande, the biggest city in Tierra del Fuego. The family of my friend Cristina Siemsen owns the nearby San Salvador estancia. At the bus terminal, I'm picked up by the estate's manager, Thomas Clement Hansen, a gray-haired man in thick-rimmed glasses, a wool jumper, and low-slung jeans. I throw my backpack onto his pick-up truck, and we make our way along the deserted, dusty, winding country roads of the Pampas. The only thing we see along the way is a few dry yellow shrubs; many of the water holes have dried up.

The biggest estate, Maria Behety, comes into view, a great cloud of dust in the distance. As we get close, we hear the calls of the blue-overall-clad gauchos, the cracking of their whips, the barks of their dogs. We watch them as they herd—on foot, on horseback, or on small motorbikes—hundreds of sheep into enclosures with the help of their sheepdogs. Densely packed, body to body, the sheep run through the narrow gates to the large buildings. It's shearing season here, work done by nomadic workers who every September start making their way from the Pampas, north of Buenos Aires until they reach the south of the country in January. On a ramp in a huge storage barn stand dozens of bales of compacted wool, each weighing around three hundred kilos, the work of just one day. There are around two thousand sheep here. We watch how they are rounded into smaller pens, how the shearer grabs them one by one, shears them and pushes them, shorn and naked, through a hatch, back to the outside world.

Thomas is in a rush because the next day he has to round up his own herds at the Rio Grande to count and vaccinate them. The farm he manages turns out to be somewhat run-down; the paint is peeling off all the walls; doors, windows, and fences hang wonkily on their hinges. The wind whistles through the cluster of crooked houses and the farmhouse lies empty. The men seem lost and haggard. This is Argentina as it was a hundred years previously—the self-exalting land of wandering gauchos, built on the backs of workers.

A few weeks later I arrive in Buenos Aires, and I'm immediately taken with the city. With its long *avenidas* along the river, it seems to me to be a wonderful mixture of New York and southern European cities like Madrid. I stroll down the Avenida Corrientes and discover the history of the area around the former Abastos marketplace, the neighborhood of the tango singer Carlos Gardel, today home to a modern shopping center. The corner of Corrientes and Callao is a hotspot for record shops, second-hand bookshops, theaters, and cinemas; since 1968 the students have been meeting at the Café LaPaz. I reach the old district of San Telmo and take refuge at the Café Aconcagua to read and write. On my walks over the next few days, I keep landing in La Boca, the colorful former docklands where many Italian immigrants settled and where today, in the midst of the wooden houses, stands La Bombonera, the stadium of the football team Boca Juniors, home of Diego Maradona, Juan Riquelme, and many other stars. Shipwrecks litter the riverside of the Riachuelo, which here flows into the Rio de la Plata and which holds the dubious honor of being one of the dirtiest bodies of water in the world. This was once the country's seafaring center. At the harbor's end, I find a corner house, standing detached and alone. Not a wooden house like the others in La Boca, not as brightly painted as the ones in the postcards, but a multi-storied building in a Gründerzeit style. The peeling white exterior had layers of patina; on the ground floor, you can still see the sign of a restaurant that had long closed down. I start dreaming about living here.

Shortly before I leave, I meet Cristina Siemsen. She's the daughter of an old friend from Berlin, Pieter Siemsen. Pieter's father, the socialist writer and theorist August Siemsen, had taken refuge in Buenos Aires with his family in 1936 after fleeing the Nazis and had produced the exile journal *Das Andere Deutschland*, which championed radical socialist and anti-Stalinist views. Peter, born in 1914, had soaked up the whole atmosphere of the Weimar Republic's organized workers' movement. He was active in socialist youth organizations and visited leftist colleges. Later, in Argentina, he was part of the trade union movement and the anti-fascist resistance, married, and had two daughters, Anna and Cristina. In 1952 he returned to Germany, first to the West and later moving to East Germany.

I sit with Cristina in a café in the neighborhood of Belgrano, so closely linked to the history of Jewish and anti-fascist exile in this country. We speak about her father, who had left her and her sister to go build something new back in Germany.

I met Pieter through my old friend from the Latin America Information Center in Bonn, Gert Eisenbürger, who several times helped me make connections that would prove fateful. Gert and I want to write Pieter's biography together. Pieter is a unique figure, his life story is one in which the central themes of the twentieth century collide; he embodies all the political awakenings and mistakes, the hopes and the disappointments. Now and then I go to visit him and his third wife, Lily, in their small apartment in Baumschulenweg in Berlin-Treptow, or in their little summer cottage in the Brandenburg countryside. Pieter, a slender man in his late seventies, rises with some difficulty from his armchair, greeting me in his usual attire of a baggy jumper, tracksuit bottoms, and slippers. This is in stark contrast to his neatly combed white hair and genteel facial features that give him a refined look. Then he turns to get a cup of coffee, a glass of sparkling wine or a cigarette, and we start talking.

He talks at length about how the end is nigh, especially for his health. And we fight. No conversation with him is complete without a fight—usually, we argue about why he had become such a doubter. Pieter is disappointed by his life. "I achieved nothing," he says. He is disappointed by the state of society and what he experienced in East Germany, a country for which he once had such high hopes. Under its real socialism, bureaucracy quashed the life out of public engagement and political activism, he says. He feels it took him too long to recognize this. He doubts himself, and the world, and has lost a part of his hope. And that's what I'm not willing to accept.

And yet I do understand him in moments like these. Pieter is forty years older than me, but we are both concerned with the same questions, especially concerning how best to deal with failure. It's the first time I've ever been able to speak like this with someone his age. I will end up meeting his daughter more often over the next years. For this nomad, Buenos Aires will become a place to return to again and again.

"Have you heard about Pinochet?"

Oh, my God. Not him again. Not Pinochet. Not this early in the morning. Not ever. Pinochet? Pinochet? I was sick of Pinochet.

"Pinochet?"

. . . "He's been arrested in London," she said. "Last night. Scotland Yard, acting on an order from a Spanish judge."

I thought to myself, my mind automatically switching into the Spanish I bizarrely shared with General Pinochet: *Esto tiene que ser un sueño*. This has to be a dream.

Ariel Dorfman, *Exorcising Terror:*
The Incredible Unending Trial of General Augusto Pinochet

THE MOTHERS OF THE PLAZA DE MAYO

BUENOS AIRES, 1999

Over the course of the 1990s, our Berlin law firm started to become established. We had plenty to do; as progressive lawyers, we worked on lots of criminal cases and labor law issues for workers, but without earning a great deal of money.

One sad continuity in our work: over the years, we kept finding ourselves representing victims in criminal proceedings against right-wing radicals on trial for racist violence and attacks on punks and leftists. I ended up traveling to Magdeburg over a hundred times. I hated the city's architecture just as I hated the indifference it showed after the murder of the young punk Torsten Lamprecht in May 1992. I spent endless days at the trial of the Neo-Nazi Group SSS (*Skinheads Sächsische Schweiz*) in Dresden, a group similar in its structures and ideology to the more recently active National Socialist Underground, whose victims are now being represented in an ongoing trial in Munich by lawyers who not long ago were trainees of mine.

During this time I traveled several times to Turkey as a trial monitor on behalf of German lawyers' groups and the Berlin bar association, and at one point I led a delegation to Belarus. But overall my legal work was limited to Germany. At no point during my studies or my apprenticeship was it foreseeable that I would one day apply my qualifications outside of Germany and outside of the traditional domestic legal paths. Law students who wanted to work outside of Germany applied to one of the big international law firms, became a diplomat, or went into academia. Those who wanted to fight for the enforcement of human rights and a new world order could at most engage in political activism, for instance as part of the solidarity movement. Even during my trip to Mexico and Guatemala in 1990 there wasn't much meaningful work for a German lawyer to do in the Latin American human rights movement. As a politically active person in Berlin, one could go to protests, write articles and petitions and monitor trials, but as a lawyer, there was little to be done. Undertaking transnational legal work was almost unimaginable to me—until I started working on a case that brought me back to the city I'd longed to return to since my first visit: Buenos Aires. This trip would be a first for me in my legal career and would end up changing my life.

***

It's a summer's afternoon in February 1999, and I'm sitting in the back seat of a taxi that is crawling through the heavy Buenos Aires traffic. I had taken the ferry over from Montevideo; it was delayed, and now I'm an hour and a half late, not something that would generally elicit much of a remark from a Porteño, a Buenos Aires resident. But the woman I'm due to meet in the Calle 3 de Febrero in the Belgrano neighborhood is no ordinary Porteña. Ellen Marx was born in Berlin in 1921, and the frail, stooped, white-haired woman has still maintained some Prussian traits after all these years. Even her apartment looks more like Berlin-Charlottenburg than Latin America, with German books everywhere you look. "Come in quick, we have a lot to talk about!" she says by way of greeting, and that's what we do, over a meal of sausages and potato salad. She lets me get away with being late. I'm her lawyer, and it's my job to bring about German criminal investigations into the case of her daughter, Leonor Marx, known as Nora, who was kidnapped by the Argentine military on August 21, 1976.

In March 1976 the junta, led by Jorge Rafael Videla, seized power in a putsch and proceeded to obliterate a large part of the Argentine Left. Trade unionists, students, and oppositionists (actual and purported) were arrested, brought to secret locations and tortured. By 1982 almost thirty thousand had disappeared. After the dictatorship came to an end, history was made: the democratically elected president Raúl Alfonsín created an independent committee to examine court records and other documents and investigate the fate of those who were missing. This truth commission published its report under the title *Nunca más—Never Again*. On the basis of this work and further investigations by prosecutors, members of the junta were charged and put on trial. Over the course of 1985 and 1986, they were convicted and given long prison sentences—an unprecedented move at the time.

Following the Nuremberg war crimes tribunals, the United Nations agreed on a series of human rights conventions: the Genocide Convention, the Geneva Conventions, the Torture Convention, and the Covenants on civil and political and economic, social, and cultural rights. Torture and crimes against humanity were forbidden. But during the span of the Cold War, there weren't any judges to whom victims could turn and who could convict those responsible. Grave crimes were committed in many countries but went unpunished. That's why Argentina's junta trial was so significant.

As prosecutors in Argentina continued this work and sought to put other military figures on trial, the country's armed forces, which remained powerful, threatened another putsch. The government passed amnesty laws, heralding the start of two decades of impunity. But the Argentine human rights movement kept fighting, despite the political situation. The grandmothers and mothers of the disappeared, the Madres de Plaza de Mayo, held protests every week in front of the president's palace. One of the women was Ellen Marx. Her lawyers continued to pursue her court case in Argentina and at the Inter-American

Court of Human Rights based in San José, Costa Rica. The movement grew in the 1990s as another generation joined the mothers' demonstrations: the children of the disappeared, who had now formed their own organization. They are more radical and use different methods, and their public interventions are in part aimed at challenging the continuity between dictatorship and democracy. At their demonstrations, they seek direct confrontation with police forces and the conservative elements of the public. They gather in what they call *escraches* (which comes from a Buenos Aires underworld slang word meaning "to drag out") in front of the houses of prominent generals and torturers who managed to escape punishment on account of the amnesties. The activists include a group of young artists, the Grupo Arte Callejero, who developed a logo with the simple but powerful motto Juicio y Castigo, Justice and Punishment. I will later become friends with them along with many other artists working on these issues.

The amnesties are fought in the courtroom as well as on the streets. Since the mid-1990s lawyers and Argentineans in exile have been bringing cases against the Argentine military to courts in France, Italy, and Spain. This was a first. Previously it had always been states who had carried out criminal proceedings, like those against Adolf Eichmann or the Argentine junta. The survivors and victims played only a minor role as witnesses, if at all. Now they were acting as independent protagonists in the criminal proceedings. What was also new was that the lawyers were relying on the principle of universal jurisdiction: if no prosecutions were pursued in the state where the crimes were committed, they turned to the domestic courts in other countries, even where there was no territorial link to the crimes and no nationals of that state were involved as victims or perpetrators. Spanish courts in particular broke new legal ground. Investigations were opened in Spain after human rights activists submitted a criminal complaint addressing the Chilean military dictatorship and lawyers substantiated the claims with witness testimony and documents. In October 1998 the Spanish investigating judge Baltasar Garzón issued an international arrest warrant for the former dictator Augusto Pinochet. Pinochet was in London at the time and was duly arrested. A turning point in the protection of international human rights had been reached.

It was a different story in Argentina, where criminal proceedings against the military almost ground to a complete halt in the 1990s. Supported by Nobel Peace Prize Winner Adolfo Perez Esquivel, Ellen Marx and the other mothers pushed for efforts in Germany to bring about criminal proceedings against the Chilean and Argentine military along the lines of the Spanish investigations. In early 1998, NGOs, church groups, lawyers, and Latin America solidarity groups based around the Nuremberg human rights center joined forces to form a network. This group, the Coalition Against Impunity, wanted to push for trials in Germany in cases concerning the roughly one hundred known German victims of the dictatorship in Argentina. It was this group that asked me to travel to Argentina after other lawyers had submitted the first criminal complaints in summer 1998. There had never been a complaint like this in Germany, although legally the possibility had existed for a while in cases in which Germans were victims of crimes abroad. Politically, such proceedings had no prospect of success in West Germany during the dictatorship in Argentina. The only ones in Germany registering outrage at the crimes of the junta at the time were Amnesty International, the small Latin America solidarity movement, and a few representatives from the Social Democratic Party. West Germany sold weapons and nuclear power plants to Argentina, while the social-liberal coalition under Helmut Schmidt remained as passive as the German diplomats on the ground and the mainstream media, if not perhaps even supporting the dictatorship's objectives.

I talk for hours with Ellen Marx; the seventy-eight-year-old is a lively conversationalist. Despite the big age gap and our very different life situations, we get on well, jumping from one topic to the next. Every so often she pulls more documents out of her files, answering my questions about the different cases, especially Nora's, and about the hopes she has for the criminal complaint. By the end of this first meeting, I've been well briefed.

Nora Marx is one of the four Jewish-German victims whose relatives I'm representing at that time. The others are Juan Miguel Thanhauser, Nora Oppenheimer, and Walter Claudio Rosenfeld. Relatives of German and German-descendant disappeared persons started to join together back in 1976 and 1977, during the worst years of repression. Around this time Ellen Marx, who had come to Latin America by ship in 1939 to escape the Nazis, was making frequent visits to police stations, army barracks, courthouses, and ministries, which was how she met Annemarie Zieschank, who was searching for her son Klaus. The backgrounds of the two women couldn't have been more different. When she was younger, Zieschank had been a member of the Hitler Youth girls' movement. And yet the two linked up and joined forces with other German families. They found a welcome and support not at the German embassy, for instance, but instead at the Protestant church in La Plata, which was set up in the nineteenth century as a religious community for German-speaking immigrants. They've been having regular meetings there at its headquarters in Belgrano ever since.

I join them for their next meeting. The group is almost entirely made up of women—partly because they wanted to make it less of a target for the military, and partly because lots of the men had already died or didn't have the strength their women had. And so I sit among these older ladies, and the cakes and drinks they've brought along. I introduce myself and the work we're doing, explain how the legal procedures work in Germany, and try to get to know the women. Ellen Marx moderates the gathering in an understated, matter-of-course way with her unique air of authority.

Alongside Ellen Marx, the most active member of the group is Aída Kancepolsky Rosenfeld. Her son, Walter Claudio Rosenfeld, and his girl-friend disappeared, as did their child who was born in detention along with hundreds of other children of those arrested. These babies were taken by military families or those close to the military. With the aid of state bureaucracy, the stealing of children was given legal cover through adoption. A new organization was set up to track down these children, made up of the grandmothers of the Plaza de Mayo, in which Aída is active—together with Elsa Oesterheld, the widow of the prominent Argentine cartoonist Héctor Germán Oesterheld who was kidnapped by the military along with his four daughters and their husbands and were never seen again. Oesterheld is the author of the 1957 graphic novel *El Eternauta,* which is well known by everyone I know from Argentina. In the book, he lays out a bleak vision that dramatically foreshadows the fate of his country and his own family. Elsa concisely describes the story of her family in a heart-wrenching way. She has a big dining table, she says, where she used to sit, eat, and drink with her husband, their four daughters, and their husbands; now she sits there alone.

Marcelo von Schmeling, who is the image of a young Maradona, is the youngest and loudest of those present. He was ten years old in 1976 when his father, a senior cadre in the left-wing Peronist group the Montoneros, was kidnapped by the military for the first time. They took Marcelo away, too, and later came for his grandparents, but they managed to get free and heeded their family's advice to go into hiding in exile. Then Marcelo's father and his sixteen-year-old sister Sonja dis-appeared for good. To this day there is no indication as to which of the secret detention centers they were held in.

None of them expect much of Germany. They have been disappointed too many times before. And yet they insist that we exhaust all possible legal avenues. We discuss ways of accessing information, the prospects of a legal win, the political climate in the country, and potential supporters in Argentina and Germany. The group is not interested in using the privileged access to German courts to win justice only for the "German" victims. They see themselves as part of a bigger movement fighting to learn the truth about what happened to all thirty thousand of the disappeared. They always managed to set aside political differences within the group, and that has made them strong. This approach—it's about everyone, not just the individuals involved—is typical of the human rights movement in Argentina, but it also presents its own problems, as I gradually discover. For instance, the sexual abuse of many women in detention is never addressed, not just due to shame but also to avoid singling out one particular group of victims for special treatment. I am confronted with the same argument when the debate turns to Jewish victims.

With the limited resources at my disposal, I start to research the background of the cases entrusted to me. Nora Marx, born in 1948, was already politically active by the sixties. Following some anti-Semitic incidents, she joined a Zionist self-defense group. Her mother doesn't tell me this part of the story, nor that Nora was later active in the Montoneros. This I learn from Cristina Siemsen and other friends of Nora. Ellen tells me only that Nora was a meteorologist at the National Weather Service and a trade union member, and that she was also active on behalf of women in poor neighborhoods. It's an old habit: the mothers are careful not to speak openly about their children's political militancy; they want to avoid encountering disapproval. I can understand this, but I also find it problematic since then the political identity of the disappeared—the thing that made them unique and the reason they were persecuted—risks being lost.

On August 21, 1976, five months after the military putsch and at the high point of the wave of repression, Nora had arranged a trip to the cinema, but she never turned up there, nor back at home. Ellen Marx began doing some research and, like many mothers at the time, made her way around police stations, barracks, and various authorities only to be rebuffed at every turn. There must have been some compelling reason, she was told, for her daughter's arrest. Eventually, she found relatives of two people who had been kidnapped along with Nora and from them learned some details of the arrest, that she was caught in a so-called mousetrap, which means that the police observed a meeting of her with her comrades and arrested and tortured the whole group. But the others were later released and could tell the story about Nora's arrest and her first days in a torture prison. That was all that she ever found out.

Ellen Marx speaks with what I see as a remarkable detachment about the fate of her daughter. Maybe it's because of my role as her lawyer, or maybe this kind of approach is necessary in order to survive and withstand all that she has gone through: Nora's disappearance, her son Daniel's death in an accident in Israel, and the extermination of a large part of her family by the Nazis. And she does more than just withstand it; she does not sit idly by, accepting her lot. She seizes the initiative and takes on the responsibility for herself and for others—because she is able to shoulder that burden.

I find some documents in the archives of the truth commission, my starting point for a lot of further research. Some of the most informative documents are copies of the habeas corpus applications submitted by lawyers and relatives during the dictatorship period. In taking these actions, they were trying to persuade the courts to reveal where and why the missing were being held, and to review their detention. The applications were based on the few facts that they were able to gather at great personal risk but were rejected by the court in almost every case.

At the time it wasn't clear if the submissions would ever have any kind of impact, but the applicants took legal action anyway, despite the meager chances of success. It was the right thing to do, as it subsequently became clear. A lot of the names of victims became known thanks to these applications, and the files provided some clues as to where people were held, who was involved, and who could act as witnesses.

This was also true in the case of Nora Marx. In addition to a complaint brought by her mother, I find witness statements from those who were arrested along with Nora on that August day in 1976. A meeting was due to take place in a workshop in Mataderos, the slaughterhouse district. The police had monitored the house, waited until all had arrived, arrested those present, and taken them to a nearby police station where they were tortured. Ellen had visited this very police station a few days after Nora's disappearance.

Based on the testimonies in the file, I track down others who were arrested that day and interview them. The results are frustrating. None of them know why they survived but Nora didn't. Because of Nora's Jewish heritage and her name? The Argentine armed forces not only saw themselves as carrying on the tradition of the Prussian Army but also looked favorably on the Wehrmacht and cultivated an aggressive anti-Semitism. A poem written by the father of one of the disappeared reads:

> When they gave my son his ration of beatings,
> Juan Miguel, his Jewish friend, got a double ration
> When my son was handed out his share of terror,
> His Jewish friend got a double portion
> When they had killed my son, they were disappointed to discover
> That they could kill his Jewish friend only once.

I speak with human rights organizations; many have their own archives. But we can't find any evidence to show that after being brought to the police station Nora Marx ended up at another location such as one of the secret torture centers; she may have been killed after just a few days in detention. I meet Jorge Watts, a walking archive of the human rights movement. He collects all the available information, including witness statements from former detainees, to reconstruct the topography of the hundreds of detention centers strewn all across the country and to piece together the stories of those held there. Jorge himself was held at the El Vesubio prison alongside Juan Miguel Thanhauser, whose case I was now also handling and whose father wrote the poem cited above. Jorge tells how Juan Miguel and a group of others were prepared for *traslado*, or "transfer;" this indicated that a detainee would be murdered: shot and buried in mass graves or drugged and thrown into the sea.

I ask Jorge: "Why were you not transferred along with the others?" I can sense the significance of this question. It implies that there may have been a rational logic behind the military's method of selection that the detainees could recognize. And it touches on a sensitive issue for those who survived: their sense of guilt.

Jorge gives an answer that stops me in my tracks. He says that by that time the military had tortured him so much that he lay in the corner of his cell, unable to move.

In moments like these, I can feel that I too have overstepped an inner boundary. The more I ask, the more responsibility I bear. The more I learn, the more I become involved. We talk about the past, but the conversation creates a situation in the present, one that brings together both partners in the dialogue. I am being entrusted with information and stories, and I must handle them carefully. One woman I speak to says that talking about it helps her to overcome the past—but only when there is openness on both sides.

***

In June 1999, having processed all the information, I submit four criminal complaints. Just a few weeks later it looks like the case might already be brought to a close. There are legal complications: the prosecution in Nuremberg can only investigate if the victims are German. The Jewish families I am representing were stripped of their German citizenship by the Nazis in 1941. After the war, the authors of Germany's new Basic Law, or constitution, didn't automatically reinstate the citizenship of those who fled Germany, partly because a lot of those who had been denaturalized didn't want their German citizenship back. West Germany offered to restore the citizenship of such persons on request. Of those who took up this offer, many waited for decades before submitting a request. The children of those who had emigrated—including those of Jewish-German descent who disappeared—were Argentinean because that's where they were born.

When I hear that the prosecutors are planning to close the proceedings, I draft a letter to my client. I try to break it to her as gently as possible that the case we had launched with such high hopes might now be ended prematurely. I use terms like "don't be alarmed," "it's possible," "there's a chance that." It's a convoluted letter since I also don't want to dash all hopes completely. In response, I receive a memorable fax. Ellen Marx writes: "Dear Sir"—she keeps up this formal tone throughout—"we are old and hardened fighters." She tells me I don't need to worry about her descending into hysterics, that I should just carry on working. She says that over the past twenty years she's gotten used to defeat.

The fax is an eye-opener, an important moment for me. I realize that I've fallen victim to my own prejudices. I don't talk to my other clients— the pacifist who blocks a street or the environmentalist who climbs up power station smokestacks—the way I talked to these older ladies. These women have a wealth of experience, greater than we can imagine, in dealing with repression. The image of these patient, seemingly apolitical mothers—humble and close to despair in white headscarves as they call on the regime to show mercy—was a powerful political weapon. In this way, they had stood up to the dictatorship during its most violent phase, an act of defiance that had cost some of them their lives.

The fax from Ellen Marx shames me. I should have known better, particularly with her, someone who has lost so many people and who is one of the strongest and most intelligent women I have ever met. I realize that there are some things that must be done regardless of their chances of success. Doing everything possible to uncover the truth and achieve justice on behalf of the mothers of the disappeared is one of those duties. It doesn't matter what judges, prosecutors, or other lawyers might think of me. And I learn that humility is no bad trait, especially when, as with the mothers, it goes hand in hand with persistence and a fighting spirit.

So I write to the prosecutor in Nuremberg and set out my arguments once again. The Coalition Against Impunity starts to mobilize supporters within the Protestant and Catholic churches and in the Green Party; the justice minister Herta Däubler-Gmelin and other high-profile lawyers work to bring about the opening of investigations. Our efforts are rewarded: the Bavarian Ministry of Justice assigns several prosecutors to the forty cases we submitted. Originally I was working on four of these cases; in the meantime, that number has risen to around a dozen. Before this, the prosecutors had asked us, in disbelief, if we really expected them to start investigations into events that unfolded thirty years ago in Argentina. Now they're getting reams of Spanish files translated into German and are starting to hear evidence from survivors, witnesses, and relatives, including Ellen Marx. They're also hearing witness evidence at the German embassy in Buenos Aires. What the prosecutors are reading and hearing about does have an impact; events that had seemed so distant start to feel a lot closer. We have set things in motion.

THE DISAPPEARED TRADE UNIONISTS OF MERCEDES-BENZ

BUENOS AIRES, 1999

When Chile's ex-dictator Pinochet was arrested in London in 1998 on the basis of a warrant issued by a judge in Madrid, some leftists accused the Spanish courts of neocolonialism. Like many human rights activists from Latin America, we rejected this criticism. As with Guatemala, I saw the impunity in Chile and Argentina as something debilitating for the whole society and which served to reinforce the old order. Still, it was and is right for us to always take a critical look at the politics of our work. Postcolonial theorists like the Kenyan-American lawyer Makau Mutua can help us in this. Mutua accuses people in the human rights field of constructing three categories: victims, perpetrators, and saviors, with this last category reserved solely for the West. If we work to bring about legal proceedings concerning crimes like those of the Argentine military dictatorship and in doing so focus solely on the old military figures that have long fallen from power, then we are guilty of the oversimplification that Mutua criticizes. The accused would appear in court as some evil "other," protagonists in acts of isolated excesses. This makes violence something abstract. Victims, perpetrators, saviors—these roles leave no room for political analysis and even less room for addressing the responsibility borne by Western actors.

Human rights violations are always part of a broader political and regional context, and that's the only way to properly understand the military dictatorship in Argentina. The Cuban revolution, the student movement, and strong indigenous and trade union movements triggered a growing fear of leftist and socialist projects among the elites in Latin America and the United States. The 1960s and '70s saw the rise of the National Security Doctrine, with military forces seizing power and setting up regimes of terror all across South America—in Argentina, Brazil, Peru, Bolivia, Paraguay, Chile, and Uruguay. The United States coordinated the international pursuit of oppositionists through Operation Condor, in which all the above countries except Peru also played a role. In Argentina, the organized workforce threatened the efforts to brutally enforce neoliberal politics; opposition was violently suppressed. This was accomplished not just by the military and their allies in the United States; many corporations also became willing accomplices in the persecution of trade unionists. The Argentine Truth Commission's *Nunca Más* report did mention some of these cases of corporate complicity, including that of Ford and Azúcar Ledesma. Most cases, however, remained cloaked in secrecy.

I speak about this with the Uruguay-based German journalist Gaby Weber during my visit to Buenos Aires in early 1999. We both agree that it's not enough to look at the local perpetrators, that it's crucial to also address the role played by Western entities. Our discussion prompts Weber to research whether there was any involvement of German companies that had close business links with the dictatorship.

Six months later she presents the results of her research on German radio. Her findings cause a serious stir when it emerges that West Germany's flagship company, Daimler-Benz, was involved in the crimes of the dictatorship. At the Mercedes-Benz Argentina factory in

Gonzáles Catán, close to the capital city, almost the entire independent workers' council fell victim to the repression. The workers had organized, independent of the corrupt official trade unions, to fight for better wages and working conditions. Fourteen of them disappeared between 1976 and 1977, and there was evidence indicating that the company had links to the state organs of repression. The former head of the nearby police station where workers were tortured was soon afterward appointed head of security at Mercedes. After the dictatorship ended, he was convicted of taking the baby of a murdered couple.

In Gaby Weber's radio piece, one surviving member of the workers' council, Hector Ratto, describes how, before his arrest in August 1977, he was brought to the office of Juan Tasselkraut, the company's production manager. While he waited to be taken away by the military, he witnessed how Tasselkraut gave the military the address of Diego Núñez, one of his colleagues from the council. That night Núñez was arrested at home and disappeared.

This was aiding and abetting murder. In an interview, Tasselkraut had previously said he knew what the military did with the people it arrested. On the basis of Gaby Weber's research, I take up this case in addition to those of the German-Jewish disappeared, and in October 1999 I file a criminal complaint against the German-Argentinean Tasselkraut.

This time the case does not have the full support of the Coalition Against Impunity; some of the church groups have concerns. The company is too powerful, they say, to pick a fight with. And first, they have to check with their bosses to see if Mercedes is one of their sponsors. Ellen Marx and other mothers in Buenos Aires are critical of this position. In the end, I submit the complaint in the name of the Republikanischer Anwaltsverein (Association of Republican Lawyers), a German alliance of leftist lawyers of which I am a board member.

On my next trip to Argentina, I meet some of the old trade unionists. I visit Hector Ratto and his family in their small house in a modest
working-class neighborhood in Lomas del Mirador in the countryside
outside of Buenos Aires. I am impressed by Ratto and his family. The
years of struggle have been etched onto their faces and bodies. Yet they
are open and happy to talk, and they have stayed true to their class
consciousness. The torture by the military has ruined Hector's health;
the electric shocks have left him with a damaged hip and lopsided gait.
But after his release from detention, he had to keep doing physically
demanding work to provide for his family of three daughters. He's not
the type to indulge in big rhetoric. For him it's clear why standing up
for workers' rights was the right thing to do. As a result, he and his colleagues in the workers' council were tortured, and many of them were
murdered—crimes that nobody, including the German Mercedes trade
unionists, had taken any interest in then. But he doesn't complain.
Without any great pathos, he simply tells what happened.

The German broadcaster ARD is planning a short program on the
disappeared trade unionists, and Hector and I are invited for an interview in a small studio in downtown Buenos Aires. Hector arrives after
a long day at work and his journey home afterward will take over an
hour. I talk to the TV people and insist that they provide a car to bring
him home, but Hector vehemently refuses to accept this privilege. After
the interview, he sets off on the long journey home by bus.

The case causes a stir in Germany. Mercedes denies the accusations
and refuses to comment on account of the ongoing investigation. We try
to mobilize public support for the surviving trade unionists. And so,
a few months later in spring 2000, I find myself in Buenos Aires once
again. The magazine Spiegel's prominent Latin American correspondent Matthias Matussek is due to join me. My initial impression of him
is as a surly and cynical man who has to let everyone know that in this

part of the world, he embodies the vast power of his publishing house. I spend two days working with him and his photographer. Eventually, Matussek gets drawn into the story—helped along by meeting Ellen Marx, who serves him her German potato salad with sausages.

We travel to the Argentine headquarters of Mercedes-Benz, and at reception, Matussek demands to speak to one of those responsible. They're not available, we are told; Matussek presses them on the point but is still fobbed off. When we start taking photos, security escorts us from the premises and forces us off the pavement in front of the building, so we move to the other side of the ten-lane Avenida del Libertador.

When Matussek has written up the story, I read a draft, which runs to several pages, to check some facts. He begins with his phone call to the press office of the company's German headquarters in Untertürkheim and how they reacted to his request: "That's old news, why are you interested in that?" The article looks set to attract a lot of attention, but it's pulled from publication at the last minute. This is not surprising if you flick through *Spiegel* and see the number of Mercedes ads. In the end, they publish a much shorter piece with a very different focus.

***

The press attention and the legal proceedings in Germany prompt the former Mercedes workers and workers' councils in Buenos Aires to join forces again. Things also start to develop in the national courts: Argentine lawyers challenge the amnesties with some success—though there are still no criminal proceedings. Then the Inter-American Court of Human Rights rules that after such serious crimes, states have an obligation to at least try to clarify what happened through legal proceedings. Courts in Argentina heed this ruling, and soon a "truth tribunal" is set up in the provincial capital La Plata, about an hour from

Buenos Aires. I attend one of the hearings that is looking at the procedures within Mercedes. Everything looks as it would at a regular trial:
the judges' bench, the prosecutors, third-party plaintiffs and their lawyers. The public gallery is quite full. Here the state is providing a forum
in which the survivors of the violence and the relatives of the dead
can be heard: an important first step in overcoming trauma, trauma
borne by individuals as well as by society as a whole. All that's missing are those accused; the defendant's bench is empty. Everyone in the
room knows who should be sitting there, but for now, the suspects are
appearing only as witnesses. Former managers at the car manufactur-
ing firm squirm and stonewall under questioning.

But Mercedes faces increasing pressure. For a number of years the
German Association of Ethical Shareholders has been using the company's annual shareholders' meetings as a chance to ask questions and
give a platform to trade unionists from Argentina. Mercedes sets up
an international investigation commission, but this group never takes
the time to hear evidence from our clients, the witnesses and family
members of victims. As a result, their final report is incomplete, a mere
box-ticking exercise for the company.

The prosecutors working on the proceedings in Nuremberg do hear
evidence from Hector Ratto and other witnesses, but we don't see much
progress. The German authorities don't dare to go hard after Mercedes
and its manager, Tasselkraut. It's frustrating because, after everything
I've learned, I'm convinced that the company did make pacts with the
dictatorship. The victims' families get a lawyer to push for more criminal proceedings—this time in Argentina—and they also file a lawsuit against the company in the United States seeking compensation.
Mercedes is now forced to defend itself on several fronts. We know that
the legal actions will take years, but there is some comfort. The mighty
corporation Mercedes treats us like a pest, an annoyance—we see the

flares of arrogance in its responses. But our transnational legal action—as new for us as it for them—is causing them serious headaches.

***

The significance of our chosen approach—of looking at the political and economic background and impact of the military dictatorship—is confirmed by the events of December 19 and 20, 2001, that shook Argentina. While not utterly unexpected, nobody could have foreseen how dramatic it would be when the country's banking system collapses. Account holders can't access their money; mass protests break out. The police response is brutal; the president resigns, leaving his official residence via helicopter. The country has five presidents over the course of just a few weeks.

The sudden disappearance of the state creates a vacuum that is filled through new initiatives of all kinds. For one historic moment, there appears the entire spectrum of political opposition: neighborhood groups are formed, gatherings are held at various levels, there is widespread political participation. Workers occupy factories, the sewing company Brukmann, the Hotel Bauen, the Chilavert printers. My colleagues take legal action against the police violence. And many of the artists with whom I have become friends over the years are now doing political work; with the limited means at their disposal, they make art intended as direct political interventions.

Even as a student I never believed that the law alone could solve everything. I could always see we were merely working on one aspect of problems that were in fact much broader. At this time I experience how important it is to have various ways of seeing and perceiving the world, of interpreting and approaching reality. There is little doubt that the situation in Argentina can primarily be traced back to neoliberal economic developments since the 1970s. But how can we make this clear to people? How should we organize resistance? The questions lead to surprising parallels between us lawyers and the artists. Both art and law claim a certain amount of autonomy in society. For those of us with a critical approach, the significance of the existing political and economic power relations is quite clear; it's almost impossible to act independently of them. But economic power is not always directly reflected in the field of law or art; there are gaps and opportunities for action. The rule of thumb for the political artist and the political lawyer: we can only produce real art, or law that is truly just, if we ensure that we do not allow ourselves to be politically instrumentalized, if we follow the genuine language and logic of art or law.

***

I find the work on the Argentina cases particularly fulfilling because they bring together these different ways of approaching reality. In my work, I'm often limited to talking about the legal details, but here I am part of a debate in which the present is tied up with the past, and the law is closely linked to politics as well as the work done by artists. In 2003 we join up with the direct democracy movement Neue Gesellschaft für Bildende Kunst in Berlin to organize an exhibition and a series of events under the heading "The Everyday and Forgetting: Argentina 1976/2003." One of the artists we invite is a small, somewhat eccentric guy with a serious, concentrated air. Eduardo Molinari has created a collage covering a table and a wall in the center of the exhibition with materials from his *Archivo Caminante*, the walking archive. He cultivates the art of walking as an aesthetic practice, an interdisciplinary and collective act. The wanderer moves in ever-changing surroundings, connected with others, open for new forms of knowledge and practices. When we meet at his archive, a small room on the periphery of Buenos Aires packed full with photographs, index cards, and folders, he explains: For him, it's about chains of association that lead the way from the past—from old photos, newspaper clippings, or documents—into the future. In this way, he hopes to trigger an awareness, to show that Argentina's history can explain and account for a lot of what happened, even for those parts of history, such as the system of torture camps and disappearances, which now seem so alien and unreal.

I meet Eduardo and many others again in Cologne in 2004 at the group exhibition Ex Argentina, which examines the crisis of the years 2001 and 2002. Many of the artworks address the continuities and threads that link the country's colonial history, the neoliberal model established under the dictatorship, and a present-day still reeling from the crisis. Eduardo's installation relates to the Camino Real, an old colonial trade route for silver and gold that led from Buenos Aires to Potosí and Lima. His work reminds the viewer that the discourses that are so dominant today on civilization, progress, and free trade, and the happiness they are purported to bring are the same ones relied on by these earlier colonialists to legitimize the oppression of the indigenous peoples of Latin America.

The themes explored by the artists in the Grupo Arte Callejero are similar to my own. But while we lawyers are dependent on finding clear pieces of evidence and can act only in a few limited cases, the artists can take a much broader view in their large-scale artworks. In their cartography work—what they call militant investigations—they use graphics to link the products of transnational companies like Mercedes with those moments in history when the firms exerted massive violence to secure their profits. Thus the Mercedes limousine is shown alongside the rise of the Nazis, the Argentine military dictatorship, and the persecution of trade unionists.

***

As the new century begins, working together with political activists and artists from around the world has become a central part of my work; I couldn't imagine a life without it. My work as a criminal defense lawyer in Berlin is still how I earn my living. Every day I cycle to the criminal court in Moabit and do what I always wanted to do: defend people against the state and the reach of its criminal laws. I defend purported members of revolutionary cells accused of attempting to blow up the Berlin department of immigration in 1986 and Berlin's Siegessäule monument in 1991, though the charges are based on the evidence of a dubious prosecution witness. I still have reason to travel to the former East German states to appear as a joint plaintiff in trials of radical right-wingers. And I experience the court, where I usually appear in robes to represent others, from a different perspective. I find myself on the defendant's bench after joining an appeal to German soldiers published in the newspaper *Taz* during the Kosovo war, an action that the Berlin prosecutor sees as incitement to desertion. I'm acquitted, but the theme of the trial—the misuse of the term "human rights" in claiming that aggressive military interventions taken in the old colonialist tradition are in fact humanitarian actions—is a topic that has stayed with me ever since.

I'm active on many fronts, maybe too many. At our law firm, engaging with lawyer and civil rights networks is an important part of the ethos. I'm elected chairperson of the German Association of Republican Lawyers. Germany became more liberal during the last decades, and the situation facing left-wing lawyers has changed significantly since the group was formed during the terrorism hysteria in Germany in 1979. Colleagues who once faced threats of professional tribunals and even criminal proceedings are now established lawyers, and so we try to use our influence as an expert organization, in particular to fight measures aimed at "toughening up" criminal law and police law. For this work, we link up with similar organizations throughout Western Europe, and my work as a lawyer is also increasingly international in nature. I serve as a European defense lawyer in Warsaw, Athens, and Barcelona, and as an advisor to demonstrators from the counter-globalization movement after the brutal police actions at the summit meetings in Gothenburg and Genoa in 2001.

Largely thanks to the Argentina cases, I gradually link up with international networks of human rights organization and lawyers. Many of the lawyers are criminal defenders like me and are well used to confrontations with state power. We agree that the legal fight should continue to be fought against former dictators who still hold a lot of power, like Rios Montt in Guatemala. But many of us are not content to stop there. We want to try to broaden the scope of what we saw unfold after Pinochet's arrest in 1998. We want to extend the reach of these efforts and include powerful figures involved in contemporary human rights violations from Russia, China, and the United States. We know that it will not be easy.

"What has happened to me is merely a single case and as such of no particular consequence, since I don't take it very seriously, but it is typical of the proceedings being brought against many people. I speak for them, not for myself."

Franz Kafka, *The Trial*

SUCCESS WITHOUT VICTORY: FROM VIDELA TO RUMSFELD

NEW YORK AND BERLIN, 2004

It's August 2004, and I'm standing in front of a building on Broadway in New York City. I'm somewhat nervous because I'm about to get involved with a case that goes far beyond anything I've taken on to date. I'm here to meet Michael Ratner and Peter Weiss from the Center for Constitutional Rights, a non-profit organization that has been fighting for human rights since the sixties. So far we've only spoken on the phone but now we will meet and start working together for the first time.

The case we will discuss is a well-known one. In spring 2004, images were released that sent waves of shock and anger around the world: photos of naked Iraqi prisoners of war being abused and humiliated by US soldiers at Abu Ghraib prison. Some pictures show the torturers, including the young soldier Lynndie England, posing beside their victims. The injustice was blatant, and the world was outraged. Even President George W. Bush did not resort to his usual post-9/11 rhetoric to justify using harsh methods against the enemy. He promised investigations and criminal proceedings against those responsible, whom he referred to as "rotten apples." The soldiers from the night shift in Abu Ghraib were intended to serve as scapegoats, shielding those more senior personnel in the military chain of command.

From the look of the Center for Constitutional Rights office on
Broadway, it's easy to see that this is a space of the alternative scene:
political posters on the walls, threadbare and stained carpets, cramped
desks. This small group of lawyers is funded by private donations and
grants from big US and European foundations. They also have pro-bono
support from large law firms and universities that provide people to
help work on civil rights lawsuits. In the Anglo-American legal sphere
groups like these, most of them progressive, are an established part of
the legal system. Some, like the American Civil Liberties Union (ACLU),
enjoy a reputation built over decades and a multimillion-dollar budget.

Michael Ratner, the Center's president, is small and balding; Peter
Weiss, its vice president, is tall and gray-haired. They have invited me
to come from Berlin because they are concerned that very little has happened in the United States since the pictures were published a few months
back. While legal proceedings are ongoing against Lynndie England and
other soldiers, the government has indicated that there should be no
further investigations, especially not into more senior figures. All official reports indicate that Abu Ghraib is just the tip of the iceberg. The
torture methods shown to be in use there were exported to Iraq from
Afghanistan via Guantánamo by army forces and intelligence agencies
from late 2001 onward. Lynndie England and the others were foolish
enough to allow themselves to be photographed; that's why they're on
trial. But the humiliation and degradation of detainees—including the
sexual degradation we saw in the photos—is something systemic.

***

Following the attacks in the United States in 2001, the US administration and its lawyers declared that various groups of detainees had
no rights. It was argued that they were not covered by the Geneva
Conventions or by the human rights norms protecting the fundamental

rights of detainees. This applied initially to Taliban and Al-Qaida suspects, but after the illegal invasion of Iraq in spring 2003, thousands of prisoners of war were treated this way. The orders came from above: from the Pentagon and the government.

The Center, led by Ratner and Weiss, wants to tackle the planners and architects of this system but it seems that any action in the United States would be impossible. So they have started looking into the prospects of criminal proceedings under the principle of universal jurisdiction, independent of where the crime was committed and the nationality of the victims and perpetrators. Following what happened with the former Chilean dictator Pinochet, they hope to submit a comprehensive criminal complaint in Europe to bring about investigations of Abu Ghraib by prosecutors and judges there. The legal foundation of this approach is based on the principle of complementarity: states are obliged to investigate their own war crimes, but if they fail to do so then the international community or other states can step in and take on this task.

Ratner and Weiss turned their attention to Germany after finding an article by prominent criminal lawyers Florian Jessberger and Gerhard Werle describing the German Code of Crimes against International Law that entered into force in 2002. The new law sounds promising. It gives German prosecutors a broad scope to act in cases of war crimes and crimes against humanity, even when there is no direct link to Germany. When Michael Ratner got in touch with the authors looking for a German lawyer, Florian Jessberger gave him my name since I was familiar with this topic from my work on the crimes of the Argentine military dictatorship.

At the meeting, I remind Peter Weiss that we had met two years earlier at a conference in Moscow organized by the International League for Human Rights. Weiss, who is seventy-nine when we meet in New York, was seen as a legend by the rest of us at the conference. He was one of the first to very successfully use international law as a tool to enforce human rights. Weiss is Jewish and fled from Vienna in 1938 to the United States via Czechoslovakia and France. Toward the end of the war, the US Army needed German speakers and asked Weiss to help with the interrogations of high-ranking German prisoners of war. At our meeting, he recalls that period: "We didn't torture even the Nazis, those who were guilty of such terrible crimes. I think we even got more information out of the detainees when we talked to them and played chess with them." At any rate, for him, it's clear: "For ethical reasons, we must not become like our enemies." When the war ended, he joined the US government's OMGUS unit in Berlin, working to investigate and break up the big German cartels that had supported Hitler and the war. He traveled throughout Allied-occupied Germany questioning people, including Hermann Josef Abs, the leading Nazi banker and banker for the new West German state, and was also involved in the preparations for the Subsequent Nuremberg Trials against industry leaders.

He later became a lawyer, earning his living with trademark law while doing voluntary work for civil and human rights. In the early 1980s, he and other lawyers from the Center unearthed a forgotten old law from 1789, the Alien Tort Claims Act. It allowed foreign nationals to sue in the United States for breaches of fundamental tenets of international law. Peter turned to this law after being contacted by relatives of Joelito Filártiga, a torture victim from Paraguay. Police officer Américo Peña-Irala, the man who murdered Filártiga, was living in the United States. The Center for Constitutional Rights brought the case on behalf of Filártiga's family, and in 1980 Peter and his team won the case on appeal. The judges deemed the torturers to be *hostis humanis generis,* enemies of all humanity, and ordered Peña-Irala to pay more than ten million dollars.

Peter made legal history with this case. He embodies a historic thread running from the breaking up of the German trusts that had supported the Nazis, to the Nuremberg trials, right up to the modern practice of human rights groups. He has always been somewhat ahead of his time. The Nuremberg principles had fallen into obscurity during the Cold War years; there were no attempts to prosecute elites of states engaged in grave injustices or industrial leaders. But after the Peña-Irala case, Alien Tort Claims Act lawsuits became a common practice. US human rights organizations used the law first to take claims against state torturers or war criminals like Radovan Karadžić, and later to sue companies involved in human rights violations or pollution such as oil firms Unocal in Burma and Shell in Nigeria. Lawyers around the world followed this example and began filing lawsuits in their own countries in response to grave human rights violations.

Peter Weiss achieved another breakthrough together with the International Association of Lawyers Against Nuclear Arms (IALANA). They managed to convince the United Nations General Assembly to seek an advisory opinion from the International Court of Justice in The Hague, arbitrator of disputes between states, on the legality of the threat and use of nuclear weapons. Here was another instance of a national or indeed supranational institution taking action thanks to the initiative of a non-governmental organization. After several years the court issued its opinion, holding that the use of nuclear weapons violates international law.

Winning these kinds of cases helps us in summoning the courage to go after the US Army for torture in Iraq. But as we get into the discussion, we ask ourselves if it makes sense to seek prosecutions in Europe. It's true that the national and international laws had changed greatly since the Second World War. Unlike at the time of the Vietnam War, it is now possible to litigate US war crimes before European courts. But the most powerful country in the world is vehemently fighting this legal development. It refused to ratify the statute of the International Criminal Court and seeks to put pressure on states that do support international criminal justice. If the German authorities reject our case out of fear of US power, do we then risk repercussions and potentially long-term setbacks?

In the end, we decide it's worth submitting the complaint. There is plenty of factual evidence to substantiate the Abu Ghraib torture allegations. It's not just the photos. Several internal investigations by US forces corroborate the claims. The methods shown in the photos and detailed in the reports qualify as torture. As a result, they may be prosecuted in Germany. And there is even a direct German link since many of the officers stationed at Abu Ghraib, and whom we hope to target with the complaint, belong to units based on German soil. So the question at the heart of the case is a political one: is the German federal prosecutor prepared to conduct criminal proceedings against high-ranking US officials? We know that we need to put forward a comprehensive and persuasive legal argument in order to have any impact on the prosecutors and the legal community and bring about a serious legal and political discussion. This is new legal ground, and not just for prosecutors in Germany.

***

The day that set all these processes in motion, September 11, 2001, also had a far-reaching impact on me personally. I had visited New York just a few days before and had strolled through the East Village and the Lower East Side with Elizabeth, my host in the city. We hopped from bar to bar, and everywhere we went she would meet people she knew, from the Mexican restaurant to the dimly lit pub on Houston Street where IRA sympathizers met. I was living my dream of a city packed with people from all over the world who feel at home in a place.

After the attacks, I check in with Elizabeth to see if she's ok. I don't hear back from her for a while, and then a long email arrives. She was living right beside the fire station from which firefighters, many of them now dead, had rushed to reach the twin towers at the World

Trade Center. Elizabeth had known a lot of them, had spoken with them. Now she was utterly despondent. The attacks had been aimed in part at that diversity we had seen on our walks in late summer.

I feared an escalation in violence and swiftly took a position against the looming wars in Afghanistan and beyond, rejecting the idea that wars could ever heal. At our law firm in the former East Berlin bohemian district Prenzlauer Berg, joint statements were drawn up with several civil right groups. Together we organized resistance to the new German anti-terror laws known as the *Schily-Paket*.

The events of the following months—the photo of suspected Taliban member John Walker Lindh naked and duct-taped, the Guantánamo detainees in orange prison uniforms with hands and feet in chains, the reports of extrajudicial killings and torture—made it clear that this was about more than just limitations of civil rights in Germany, Europe, and the United States. Now people were being gravely injured or even killed, with and without purported legal basis. We could write appeals and we could demonstrate against the war in Iraq, but the photos of Abu Ghraib left me feeling utterly powerless at first. Then the request from Michael Ratner and Peter Weiss arrived and paved the way for me to take action.

***

Michael and Peter have a lot more experience in challenging powerful states and actors than I do. But here in New York in the summer of 2004, they treat me as their equal. There is a lot to discuss. The criminal complaint is due to be submitted in Germany in three months time, in November, shortly after the US presidential elections. We want to put the new US administration—which we hope will no longer be led by President Bush—in an awkward position. Despite all our experiences to the contrary we are seeking to force them to put the torturers on trial in the United States. The United States claims to work to bring about democracy and human rights around the world. Wouldn't it thus be disastrous for their reputation and their own interests if prosecutors in other countries start addressing US war crimes?

We also discuss how best to divide up the vast amount of work. We want to evaluate several dozen reports from NGOs and the United Nations, as well as the internal investigations by US forces, and we plan to draw up dossiers on all senior military, intelligence, and political figures who may bear responsibility. This work is done by students from the universities that work with the Center—a form of cooperation I've never seen in Germany.

Also new for me is how relatively transparent the US government bodies are despite some recent restrictions. A lot of the documents we reference in the complaint were written by the administration and were obtained by journalists or through requests from civil rights organizations under the Freedom of Information Act. My job is to write the legal analysis on whether the acts in question meet the definition of torture under international and national law and whether the German authorities can take action in the case. In doing this work, I see myself not as a European taking on the United States but rather as an anti-torture activist working with US colleagues to hold those responsible to account.

We also discuss practical problems. I ask about how we should communicate from now on, whether we will be under surveillance. Michael's response: "Let's not let them get to us, even if they do read what we write." He tells me that they received hundreds of pieces of hate mail when they started defending the first detainees at Guantánamo. One of them wrote that Michael should just invite the Taliban home so they could eat his children.

I form an enduring friendship with Michael and Peter. Peter invites me to his house in the Hamptons, the weekend stomping ground of choice for wealthy New Yorkers. That's where I get to know his wife, Cora. The two of them have been staunch anti-war activists for the past half-century.

Cora is part of a global network of women's peace groups and was one of the most prominent opponents of the Vietnam War. In the early seventies, she traveled to Hanoi to lead peace talks. Peter tells an anecdote from this time about a visit from Swedish prime minister Olof Palme who was in New York for a UN meeting. At a reception in Cora and Peter's house, Palme gave a short speech against the war. Guests were able to hear the speech again later in the evening, broadcast loudly from a tape recorder in the hallway of the house next door. The FBI agents bugging Peter's house had run into technical problems, much to the amusement of all those gathered.

The United States committed widespread war crimes during the Vietnam War, but at the time the idea of domestic or international criminal proceedings against the senior officials responsible would have been inconceivable. Anti-war activists set up the Russell Tribunal, a special court of public opinion named after the English philosopher Bertrand Russell. The facts were presented, and moral judgment was passed, but there were no legal consequences. When it emerged that the United States had massacred villagers at My Lai, Peter joined forces with investigative journalist Seymour Hersh to find ways of taking legal action against the generals on behalf of the victims. In the end, they were forced to abandon the work because the government in Hanoi didn't want to recognize a US court in the middle of a war.

***

Michael's political path is closely linked to the Vietnam War. He studied law at Columbia University and in 1968 took part in the big campus protests that were brought to a brutal end by the New York police. He started working with the Center for Constitutional Rights, which, two years earlier, had been set up by William Kunstler, Arthur Kinoy, and other left-wing lawyers. Clients represented by the Center included leaders of the student movement, members of the militant Black Panther Party, and victims of police violence after the revolt at Attica prison was violently crushed. I was fascinated by how the Center's lawyers had intervened on the side of the marginalized and the weaker party in almost every chapter of contemporary US protest history. In the eighties and nineties, the Center sued the US government several times for its wars and military interventions, especially in Central America. After the September 11 attacks, the Center took on the unpopular task of representing terrorist suspects who were being held at Guantánamo without charge or any court order and who in many cases were abused while in detention.

Michael has firsthand experience of Guantánamo. In the early nineties, he had visited the prison as a lawyer when the US government was interning Haitians seeking to enter the United States and who were thought to be HIV positive. When the Center took on these new Guantánamo cases it was essentially on its own; only a handful of other left-wing lawyers were willing to get involved in the defense of the detainees. In the period directly after September 11, the mood was one of hysteria regarding terrorist attacks, and the established law firms were initially unwilling to take the professional risk. Eventually, the Center was joined by other lawyers and civil rights groups.

These are exactly the kinds of developments that the Center aims to set in motion. Its staff espouses a philosophy summed up in the title of a book by Jules Lobel, now president of the Center: *Success Without Victory*. In the book, Lobel describes how the road to political wins can be paved with legal defeats. Using examples from the history of the US civil rights movement, he shows that strategic litigation does not necessarily require success in the courtroom. A negative court decision can help to shed light on the truth and mobilize the affected communities and movements. These legal disputes can drag on for decades, so it's important to develop long-term political as well as legal strategies. The Center for Constitutional Rights takes more risks than other established organizations; in many cases, it tests certain legal tools for the first time. Many others go on to benefit from this work in future cases.

***

I fly back to Berlin, buoyed and energized by the encounters and conversations in New York. A lively transatlantic dialogue arises. I send Peter and Michael outlines and draft passages of texts for the complaint. They ask questions and make suggestions; Peter in particular reads and comments on everything. This is a challenge for me, and I often have the feeling that I'll never be able to finish. In the end, it proves to be a productive method; through the ongoing exchange, the text gains in length and authority. In three months we manage to compile the 200-page complaint, which we present to the public in Berlin on November 30, 2004.

I'm very much aware that a criminal complaint in Germany against the US secretary of defense will raise many questions. Success without victory: to German lawyers that sounds at best naive, at worst like an abuse of the law for political purposes. The legal mainstream will doubt the seriousness of the project and of the cause in general. We will be accused of filing the case just to get public and media attention. Do we really expect German prosecutors to open investigations in a case like this? Our response will be to ask: would Pinochet have been arrested in 1998 if prosecutors and judges had limited themselves at all times to the logic of the realistic and the feasible? When lawyers representing torture victims lodged those first complaints in Madrid in 1996 and judges started opening preliminary investigations, that arrest was anything but likely.

International criminal law has undergone rapid development in recent times. The UN tribunals for Yugoslavia and Rwanda were set up in 1993 and 1995, and in 2002 the International Criminal Court began its work in The Hague. The court is based on the idea that the core international crimes are "of concern to the international community as a whole" and thus no longer merely a domestic matter for the state in question.

I'm encouraged in part by our own proceedings against the Argentine military in Germany. When we brought these cases, we didn't know what could come of it, but in the end, it did have some impact. It led, for instance, to Germany issuing arrest warrants and extradition requests for former head of state Jorge Videla—and more were to follow.

Our complaint is obviously an unusual move. We acknowledge this in the text by explicitly addressing the political background. The United States and its allies are fighting a vague, almost indefinable enemy—terror—for an indeterminate amount of time and are asserting a right to use any means of warfare to do so. The idea is that in this conflict the law should yield to a political *Dezisionismus*, or decisionism, as described by Carl Schmitt in his work *Political Theology*: "sovereign is he who decides on the exception" and who legitimizes the state of emergency. If we now have a proclamation of a permanent state of emergency, this dictum impacts everyday political life. The Italian philosopher Giorgio Agamben argues that then the state of emergency is no longer based on an external, temporary situation of actual threat, and thus there is a risk that it may be confused with the norm itself. People stop thinking and adjudicating in legal categories. Importance is placed instead on what is expedient, and expedience can be asserted about anything that serves one's own security.

The worldwide moral and legal condemnation of torture took decades to establish. And yet torture continues to be a common practice in many states. The fight to eliminate it is key to the future of a humane and civilized world. For those of us who are part of this fight, this means that we challenge every situation in which torture is practiced and propagated and work to ensure that torturers and those who orchestrate torture face criminal sanctions. We see our Abu Ghraib complaint as a part of this effort.

Impunity for those who instigated the war crimes at Abu Ghraib sets a dangerous precedent. Many governments take note of the bad example set by the West and feel emboldened to continue their own— as they see it, newly legitimized—torture practices by invoking the fight against terrorism.

This is exactly the kind of situation that Robert Jackson, the American chief prosecutor at the Nuremberg Trials and one of the most important jurists of the last century, had in mind when, in his opening statement in November 1945, he said:

And let me make clear that while this law is first applied against German aggressors, the law includes, and if it is to serve a useful purpose it must condemn aggression by any other nations, including those which sit here now in judgment. We are able to do away with domestic tyranny and violence and aggression by those in power against the rights of their own people only when we make all men answerable to the law.

In his address, Jackson hit upon precisely what concerns us now: the equality of all people before the law, which is the bedrock of all justice. We want to show what happened, what led from September 11 to Abu Ghraib, from a handful of exceptions to the torture ban to the sanctioned torture of thousands of prisoners of war. We hope that this message will also be heard in Germany. We want to challenge those in Germany who seek to allow torture in exceptional circumstances—like the former Frankfurt police vice president Wolfgang Daschner in the case of the murder of a child by Magnus Gäfgen.

Reactions to the complaint prove very mixed. While the German media coverage is limited, there is extensive reporting internationally, in the United States but also in Italy, France, and Spain. We get an interesting response from Amnesty International, whose senior legal advisor Christopher Hall openly criticizes us. By applying international criminal law against such powerful opponents, he argues, we will not only lose the case but also do a long-term disservice to the laws on human rights protection. He fears that limits will be placed on the scope to bring war crimes before the courts—similar to what happened in Belgium when the laws were changed following a criminal complaint against US generals and the ensuing threats from the United States to pull the NATO headquarters from Brussels unless something was done. In response, we argue that the law is meaningless if it doesn't apply to powerful lawbreakers. We also hope to avert these dangers by submitting meticulous legal arguments and by building support for our approach. Critics from the Left accuse us of legal positivism, a kind of naive trust in the written law, of showing blind faith in the laws as they stand, thinking we can effect genuine change by using these laws and participating in this flawed legal system. Power will triumph over law, they argue. How can we not see that, they ask, are we really that naive?

Both Hall and our left-wing critics take an essentially static view of power relations. We, on the other hand, seek to change the status quo. We believe that political power is not necessarily reflected point for point in the legal sphere, that there are some disparities and ruptures, and that there are certain spaces and certain moments which we can make use of.

It's hard to know what to say when I'm asked about my personal feelings during this time. My personal views, my political position, and my profession have all merged. On one hand, this is what I always hoped for in my career. On the other, these autumn months of 2004 have been so intense that there was no time left for enjoying life. Without following any master plan, I have ended up working with a good mixture of theory and practice. But how should I deal with the fact that there will always be too much work for one person or one small group of people?

***

The US election does not turn out as we had hoped. George W. Bush takes office for the second time. The newly reinstated administration responds harshly to our efforts, labeling the criminal complaint a "frivolous lawsuit" and putting pressure on the German government to close the proceedings. Henry Kissinger, former US secretary of state and staunch defender of *Realpolitik*, is moved to comment on the case. He helped organize the Pinochet putsch in 1973 and could thus himself someday face prosecutions abroad. Now we hear that he's been warning people in Washington not to underestimate the dangers of our criminal complaint and the possible consequences. Before traveling overseas, Kissinger always contacts the relevant embassy to check that there are no actions pending against him.

Then Rumsfeld declares that he will not travel to Germany until the matter has been brought to an end. He fears he will face prosecution if he enters the country. The US administration's approach—coercing a foreign government to influence legal proceedings—demonstrates a distinct lack of understanding of state sovereignty and the separation of powers. But we never expected much subtlety from the US officials. What's more interesting for us is that they sense a personal risk. This would have been absolutely unimaginable just a few years previously. They know what they are doing, they know they are breaking the law, and they know the price they will have to pay if rule of law standards are applied. From Washington, we hear murmurings that there is a sense of fear around. Those who had seemed all-powerful, those who had appeared out of reach, are now revealed to be vulnerable.

THE STRUGGLE FOR COLLECTIVE MEMORY

PATAGONIA, BUENOS AIRES, ASUNCIÓN, 2005

I arrive in the small Patagonian town of Zapala in January 2005, a few weeks after submitting our criminal complaint against Rumsfeld. I'm here to visit Adriana Marcus, who between 1978 and 1979 was detained at ESMA, a Navy school used as a torture chamber by the junta. Hers was one of the cases I had submitted to prosecutors in Nuremberg concerning the disappearance of people of Jewish-German descent. The proceedings had been closed in August 2004 after the prosecutors held that the statute of limitations had expired. I had appealed this decision, but from a legal perspective, there was no real need for further discussions with Adriana. Something else has brought me to Zapala: I want to talk to Adriana about her personal and political history, to try to understand her militant past.

I step into a lively world. Adriana's small house—tucked away in a dusty side street of a quiet neighborhood—is full of people. Her youngest son is there with his girlfriend and three friends from his punk band, as well as two young anthropology students from Buenos Aires who are visiting to do research at the health center where Adriana works as a doctor. We barbeque and drink wine.

Adriana is head of the health center where she has worked for the last seventeen years, but she's also a kind of social worker and activist for the rights of the disadvantaged in the region. She fights to improve their access to health care; as a result, the Mapuche Indians in the nearby rural areas often come to her at the center. When Adriana got to know them, she saw that they weren't adequately organized and often got bad deals when it came to important land issues. The handful of mostly unpaid and often inexperienced lawyers that represented them were up against an armada of highly paid lawyers hired by the property owners.

Adriana's life is full of conflict: she takes on the authorities, organizes strikes of rural healthcare workers, provides first aid at protests. She spends her wages on supplies that the inept hospital administration fails to buy. All this is done in an entirely unpretentious way. This small woman with her long gray hair is the opposite of the extrovert-types from Buenos Aires. When people there talk about human rights they are often concerned only with crimes of the dictatorship; there is no mention of current problems or the issues facing indigenous people in rural areas.

Adriana's son Manuel has already run into problems with local authorities several times; the punk scene is closely monitored by police. Adriana is worried about him; he's easily provoked and gets verbally abusive toward the police. When the high school students occupied the school a few months back, Manuel was at the center of it—along with Adriana who joined in because she was worried about him. The school director tolerated the students' action and was subsequently arrested. Suddenly Manuel was nowhere to be found. Adriana was gripped by panic, the memories of her own arrest decades earlier racing through her mind. It turned out that her son had not been arrested but had gone to the police station of his own accord to show his solidarity. The continuity of resistance.

The next day we get into Adriana's old VW Gacel and drive across the country: the Patagonian steppe, a few trees, bushes, grasses, some desert, dried out riverbeds; in the middle distance, the Andes cordillera on the Argentine–Chilean border, a couple of volcanoes. We are headed for the Laguna Blanca National Park where you can find fossils, seashells petrified over thousands of years dating back to when the region was covered in ocean. The lagoon is a birdwatchers' paradise; ornithologists from all over the world come here to observe the unique waterfowl. Adriana is angry about the corrupt local government that seeks to boost tourism while destroying a lot of the area in the process. Adriana knows the plants and herbs, she points out leaves and fruits and explains their properties. She has self-published books on medicinal and other useful plants, and she gives seminars in which she and the participants make creams, medicines, and juices. She wants to socialize this knowledge, gained over centuries by the Mapuche Indians who now face discrimination. It belongs to everyone, she says, and it cannot be allowed to become the property of pharmaceutical companies with their dubious patent laws.

We sit in the shade at the side of the lagoon and drink mate. Adriana tells me about her parents, who left Germany as children in 1933. Like many German Jews from intellectual families, her parents weren't religious. They owned one of the first big department stores in the country and were patrons of expressionist painters. Later they were forced to sell the paintings to pay for the family's escape from the country. When Adriana's mother was just ten years old, she was given a ticket for a boat journey from Marseille and put on a train in Switzerland. She had no papers, so when the train crossed borders, she pretended to be asleep. Everything went according to plan until she reached Marseille and discovered that the ship she was supposed to board had already set sail. She didn't know whom to turn to for help. A German sailor and his companion, a prostitute, found her on the street crying. She was in luck: they took care of her and made sure that she got on the next ship to Buenos Aires.

I'm curious about how Adriana got involved in political activism. "At college, everyone was involved with the Left—apart from the really stupid ones and a handful of students from rich families," she explains. Che Guevara and the Cuban revolution played a big role, inspiring young Argentineans and so many others of that generation around the world.

Like Che, Adriana studied medicine, and her faculty had a progressive dean who put an emphasis on practice. Students gained practical experience by helping out at local clinics in poor neighborhoods—*villas miserias*. At university, they discussed the causes of poverty and malnutrition. Adriana got involved in the student section of the left-wing Peronist Montoneros but, like many of her fellow students, she was politically inexperienced and reliant on the cadres and stooges in the group. "The leadership decided the political path and we, the ground forces, had to implement the directives," she says. "To this day I still can't believe the way my friends and I were back then." At the height of the conflict in the early seventies, she took part in a blockade of a road junction in a part of Buenos Aires she didn't know. She had no idea of the background of the action or why these roads should be blocked. Only later did she learn that the Montonero leadership had planned blockades on several different junctions across the city. Adriana was told to set fire to petrol that had been poured on the road from the Molotov cocktails they had brought with them that hadn't worked. When she refused, she was punished for her disobedience and forced to write up a criticism of her actions—very much in the Stalinist and Maoist tradition.

From 1975 on, the political climate intensified. The progressive university heads were sacked and replaced by people loyal to the regime. A state of emergency was declared. The death squads killed oppositionists or had them disappeared. Many of Adriana's friends grew cautious; some emigrated, others moved to different parts of the country and built new lives there. And so the putsch in 1976 was not itself the major turning point, she says. The pressure had already grown in the months before. She says she expected that leftists would be jailed, and she was prepared for situations of interrogations and torture. But nobody predicted that thirty thousand people would disappear. Adriana did not back down. She agreed to give medical care to dissident fighters. The Montonero leaders believed that the brutal dictatorship had revealed the true nature of the power structures in the system. The middle class now had to make its choice; there was no in-between, no compromise. "And so they relied solely on militancy and the strength of the armed movement," says Adriana. "We, the rank and file, were instrumentalized." Her group set up an operations room that was ultimately never used. In January 1978 she met the other activists for the last time and then broke off all contact.

One Saturday in August 1978, Adriana had arranged to meet her flatmate for lunch. Adriana was in the middle of her medical training and was working as a nurse. Her friend never showed up. "The rules were clear in cases like this. I had to stop everything, contact nobody, and most importantly not show up at any familiar addresses." Her flatmate had indeed been arrested and had, under torture, given the military her address because she assumed that Adriana would stick to the rules. Adriana had always had a plan for emergencies. She intended to use her German passport to travel overland to Montevideo and then go to Germany with the help of the German embassy. But instead she did exactly what she knew she shouldn't do: she went back to her apartment with her father. The military men intercepted her there and dragged her to a car. Her father tried to drive away but was shot at and arrested along with Adriana. The soldiers brought them to a place they didn't recognize. Adriana later learned that it was the ESMA torture center. During the journey there they whispered to each other in

German and agreed on what to say under questioning. Adriana's father was released after a few hours. To this day, Adriana can't quite grasp how suicidal her actions were. "I can only explain it in terms of denial mechanisms and the guilt I felt for those who had been killed." Victory or death—this was the motto. "I hoped that nothing would happen the way one hopes not to get pregnant during unprotected sex."

She says that in some ways the arrest came as a relief. For too long she had harbored suspicions about every parked car; she would take detours, always looking over her shoulder. A woman who was detained with Adriana and who had been living underground before she was jailed described her own arrest in similar terms. She had felt the need to phone her mother and called her from a phone box in central Buenos Aires, knowing that the phones may be bugged. She told her mother that she was wearing the brown blazer her mother had given her. This was all that the military needed. A search action was launched. She died in prison.

At ESMA, Adriana lost all sense of time. Her kidnappers threatened to cut off her hands, forced her to be naked for hours on end, searched all bodily orifices for cyanide capsules, which many Montoneros carried with them. She was blinded, hooded, and shackled to the bed and forced to listen to screams and a very loud radio. One officer told her she was in a police building and that she'd be brought before the courts and given a long prison sentence. The prisoners slept, handcuffed and hooded, in the attic of the officers' mess room on foam mattresses separated by wooden walls. She was allowed to sit down only at mealtimes, with a view of a wall. She had to ask the guard for permission when she wanted to go the toilet. She would often be brought to the showers in the early hours of the morning, naked in front of the sergeants and ESMA trainees. "I was just a number, 182, my friend was 180."

In January 1979 an officer ordered her to translate a dossier on the Montoneros into German. The officers wanted to find out if they could use the detainees for their own purposes or even persuade them to switch sides. Adriana read books on the Algerian War and the re-education of Vietnamese detainees by the French, books she was given by an officer named Alfredo Astiz, who later became well known as the "Blond Angel of Death." The officers discussed philosophy, ideology, and politics with the inmates. "They wanted to test our views."

Adriana rendered many texts into German and would pretend not to be able to understand some words so that she could phone her father. This work increased her chances of surviving. "Every day was spent teetering on the brink of the abyss. In order to survive, I had to change the outside perceptions of my opinions while at the same time assuring myself I was doing the right thing." A great deal of her energy went into this deception. She had to convince not just the officers but also her old acquaintances who were now collaborating with officials. Hanging over her head the whole time was the threat from the head of ESMA, Captain Jorge Acosta, to "send her up above," i.e., to have her drugged, put in an airplane, and dropped into the sea. Toward the end of her detention, Adriana was allowed out, escorted by officers, to visit her parents. That's when she learned how badly the German diplomats were dealing with German citizens who were disappeared. Like many people searching for their relatives, Adriana's parents had gotten in touch with the German embassy. Embassy staff put them in contact with Major Peyrano, an Argentine intelligence officer from the notorious Battalion 601. The staff at the embassy in Buenos Aires let this man use one of their office rooms to talk to the families—with no supervision—and pump them for information. When Peyrano spoke to Adriana's parents, he made the absurd suggestion that they could get the army to kidnap Adriana and then bring her to Germany. After two decades, the German authorities finally confirmed these events, but never launched an official investigation or gave any explanation to the relatives of the missing.

I ask Adriana if she ever thought about running away when she was outside the prison with the officers. Her answer is as brutal as the whole awful story: "I knew they would have taken their revenge on the others. After any attempt to escape they murdered a detainee and paraded their mutilated torso in front of us."

Adriana lives in the countryside, far from the capital, so she no longer has much contact with those who were detained alongside her. When she learned that five of them had been discussing writing a book about their time at ESMA, she joined them. The book was published in 2001 under the title *Ese Infierno* (*That Inferno*). The book describes something that Adriana and the other women experienced: how, as part of the reeducation process, they were forced to accompany officers on their evening outings. They had to change clothes and put on perfume and were brought out to fine restaurants. Later they were locked up again. Miriam Lewin, who was detained before the others, and who also took part in the book, believes that this was done to show them the comforts of capitalism.

> Look at what you're missing. You could wear nice dresses, go to shows, travel, eat at nice restaurants, but instead, you're wasting your time fighting for the poor and the outcast.

While the women sat in their elegant clothes dining with the officers, they thought of their comrades back at ESMA who would be spending the evening eating old bits of bread that the rats had run all over. This is how Miriam describes her feelings:

I only knew that it sickened me, that I hated them, that it made my skin crawl to sit at the same table as them, that I found it repulsive to pretend that they had won me over, to act like I no longer cared that they had murdered the people I loved. We felt we'd rather be at ESMA than in this fancy restaurant. We craved to be back in the concentration camp, the place where we, the kidnapped, belonged.

And then Adriana tells me—and I can hardly believe it at first—how ESMA commander Jorge Acosta said to her, "See you in Nuremberg." Nuremberg, a place where people like him could be brought to justice. Even at the height of his power, he knew that he could one day end up on trial for his actions.

***

I stay with Adriana longer than planned because I'm keen to hear all of her story and not have to worry about the time like I so often do as a lawyer. I want to get to know the people at the heart of this story, to break out of the victim/helper model.

I take a bus for almost twenty-four hours through the Pampas to Buenos Aires to visit Ellen Marx and other friends, including Marcelo Brodsky, a photographer whose brother was tortured at ESMA. I meet him at the Colegio Nacional de Buenos Aires near the presidential palace. The Colegio is the city's first public secondary school in the European tradition, a venerable institution with colonnades and a small park in the courtyard, the steps a favorite place for the students to sit. The Colegio is hosting Marcelo's major work, "Buena Memoria," a biographical research project based on photos of his own class at the school in 1967. In one photo, the boys are wearing suits and ties; the girls are in blouses, blazers, and skirts. Marcelo has enlarged the photo and annotated it in bright crayon with notes on each student, a look back at their lives up to 1996.

All of us could do this with our class photos. Lost youth, lost dreams, experiences gained, dreams lived. What makes Marcelo's photo different are the red circles around the young faces of Claudio Tisminetzky and Martin Bercovich. Claudio was killed by the military in a shootout in 1975; Martin was disappeared in 1976. Other fellow students were jailed as political prisoners or went into exile. Marcelo was active in the Trotskyist Left, was shot and forced to leave the country. Martin Bercovich was his best friend, and in a poem, Marcelo imagines he is still alive. For one artwork he gathered photos of himself and Martin taken on their hikes to the Iguazú Falls: two young men in the mountains, each with a camera around their necks. The heading over the image reads: "We could be photographers."

Marcelo's younger brother Fernando disappeared in August 1979. We now know where he was taken: there is a photo of him at the ESMA torture camp. The bureaucratic, Prussian-style military officers kept careful records of their victims and even allowed detainees to be photographed. Some of the photographs were taken by Victor Bastera, also a detainee at ESMA, who smuggled the pictures to the outside world. The photo of Fernando Brodsky shows a young man looking utterly lost, signs of torture etched across his face.

Twenty years went by before Marcelo could begin to deal with the deaths of his friend and brother. He tells me how important it was for him to first build a life for himself and his family. Security, including financial security, was necessary as a way of countering the trauma of repression, fleeing, and exile. He suffered from survivor's guilt. With all the impatience of an artist on a mission and a relative of the wronged, he is anxious to ensure his brother's memory is honored.

Marcelo helped to create one of the most iconic symbols of his generation. He got involved in the politics of remembrance, working to set up the Parque de la Memoria on the Rio de la Plata. Here—in a place where immigrants from Europe once would land, full of hope, and where later the bodies of political prisoners would wash ashore after being drugged and thrown into the sea—there is now a park where artists from Argentina and beyond can exhibit their works.

Here you can see installations by the Grupo de Arte Callejero, whose members I have met many times before, most recently at the Ex Argentina exhibition in Cologne. I'm staying with two of them during my visit, Lorena Bossi and Mariana Corral. Mariana bought their house in the Parque Patricios neighborhood with the almost US$100,000 awarded to her as the daughter of one of the disappeared in a judgment from the Inter-American Court of Human Rights against the Argentine government.

At their house, I sleep in a small upstairs room. In the room, there is a coffeehouse-style table, and a copy of a letter has been placed underneath the glass table top. It was written by Mariana's disappeared father in 1977, in Café Perla del Once, where Argentina's rock scene had emerged in the late sixties.

Mariana was never able to get to know her father, Manuel Corral. Her family never spoke about what happened to him. So she was surprised when, on her seventeenth birthday, her uncle handed her a letter written to her when she was just a baby. It was about his hope that his daughter would, through this letter, be able to understand him. "My daughter," he writes, "when you've reached the right age, and I'm not there, you'll be able to better judge me and the times into which you were born without having to rely on the impressions of others." He explains that his life and those of his comrades were based on the idea of the justice they sought for the hungry, the dispossessed, and the massacred peoples of Latin America. He addressed her directly, explaining why the relationship between him and her mother did not work out, and why it wasn't possible for him to have a private life. I'm very moved when Mariana gives me a copy of the letter as a gift and shares with me this very personal story that remains a source of deep upset for her.

***

At the end of every trip to Buenos Aires, I organize a party to help ease the pain of leaving. This party is special. A well-known tango group, the Bardos Sardoneiros, are playing on Lorena and Mariana's patio. The singer is Betina Ehrenhaus, whom I got to know when I first started representing the relatives of disappeared persons with German roots. Betina is herself a survivor of torture at ESMA, and she was one of my clients in the case in Germany. Now she goes by the name of Ruth de Vicenzo and earns her living as a tango singer. Lorena dances with her dance partner—they earn their money at the city's markets as a female tango pair, still quite unusual in Argentina. It turns out to be one of the best evenings I've spent in Buenos Aires. The next morning, my last day in the city, I'm suddenly torn from sleep. My mobile rings—I had forgotten to turn it off—and I'm stupid enough to answer. A journalist from the newspaper *taz* in Berlin is on the other end of the line: he wants a comment from me on the Karlsruhe prosecutors' decision to close the criminal proceedings against Rumsfeld. This is the first I've heard of it. Still half asleep, I give him any old answer.

Later on, I read through the decision and am disappointed by it. The German government and prosecutors have caved under pressure from Washington. Donald Rumsfeld had said he would only take part in the Munich Security Conference in February 2005 if the proceedings against him were closed. The prosecutors made their decision one day before the conference, and Rumsfeld was able to travel to Munich. The decision is blatant in its political motivation. In the reasoning, the prosecutors argue that there are already proceedings ongoing in the United States—meaning the trials of Lynndie England and others—and so there was no scope for German investigations. For me, it's immediately clear that we will have to keep working on the case. The assertion that genuine investigations are already being carried out in the United States is not plausible even at this early stage; in time it will become clear to all observers that no such investigations are underway. We decide to appeal the decision, and together with Michael Ratner and Peter Weiss in New York, I start to plan the next updated complaint, based on newly released information.

***

The importance of fighting impunity for human rights violations is made all too clear the next year when, in December 2006, I travel to Asunción in Paraguay with the Argentine lawyer Rodolfo Yanzon. Here we meet Martin Almada, who for decades has been working tirelessly for human rights. He was involved in political activism during the reign of Alfredo Stroessner, one of Latin America's longest-ruling dictators, and was arrested and tortured because of this work. The dictator's henchmen then came up with a particularly appalling plan, sending Almada's fiancée one of his shirts, soaked in blood, along with a message that he had been tortured to death. She suffered a heart attack and died. Almada went into exile abroad, a hardened enemy of the dictator, and became a lawyer with the explicit aim of bringing Stroessner to trial. Since returning home in 1992, he has been one of the few lawyers in Paraguay with the courage to pursue the country's elite. He was helped by a stroke of luck: in a police building that was due to be cleared out, someone came across a dictatorship archive with lists of oppositionists who had over the course of decades been spied on and eliminated. Almada reacted quickly when he was called in: instead of taking the archive, he decided to make good use of the country's legal system and handed the documents over to prosecutors.

This archive of terror is now stored in an unspectacular modern court building. I go there to find information on the murder of Jorge Federico Tatter, one of the cases in the complaint we submitted in Nuremberg. In the 1960s, Tatter fled to Argentina to escape Stroessner, got involved in political activism there, and was arrested after the putsch as part of the transnational Operation Condor, as we later discover from the documents we find. Argentina and Paraguay joined forces to organize Tatter's kidnapping; Germany, his home country and the state his wife turned to seeking help, did almost nothing to save him.

Tatter's widow, Idalina, and their son, Jorge Federico, are already there to greet Rodolfo and me. Idalina has for all these years been one of the most active of the Mothers' group and has been a vocal critic of the German government and the German embassy. Her anger persists to this day; she cannot forgive—not the Stroessners, not the Videlas, and not the Germans who failed to help her.

During these oppressively hot days in Paraguay, I see that progress is occurring here. We visit a modest new memorial for the victims of the dictatorship at the former police station where police detainees were once subjected to torture. We are accompanied by the German ambassador in Asunción. Things are easier than they once were for Martin Almada and others seeking to address the crimes of the past. Martin has now initiated several criminal proceedings against perpetrators from the Stroessner regime. He pushes for extradition of the former dictator from exile in Brazil and never tires of digging up new information about Operation Condor and the fateful role played by the United States.

It's easy to hatch plans with Martin; he never keeps still. He, Rodolfo Yanzon, and I have all worked in our own countries to bring about legal proceedings concerning Operation Condor. Now the three of us decide to set up the Operation Anti-Condor: where intelligence services and the apparatuses of torture once worked together across borders, we will now set up a network to coordinate the legal response.

There is a long way ahead of us, as becomes clear to me one evening when we are guests at the birthday celebrations of a former prosecutor who works with Martin. The party is held at a country club, the atmosphere is dignified, the guests at the tables around to us are a curious mix. The old landowning oligarchy mingles with the new: the smugglers and the drug dealers, along with several civil servants. Paraguay is one of the most corrupt countries in the world.

Sitting opposite me is the host's wife, with dyed blonde hair and dressed in a sharp suit. She comes from a landowning family and is clearly part of the social milieu that gathers in the club. But then, with considerable emotion, she tells me the story of how she and her husband were cast out from the centers of power and are still only just tolerated here. Her husband was assigned to work on investigations into the smuggling of cars stolen in Brazil. When he followed the trail, it led him to the highest circles of government in Paraguay. At first, they were lenient with him. He got some tip-offs from friends, all low-key. But he continued investigating, and one day some strangers picked up his children from school and dropped them home. The message was clear. He left his job and has worked as a lawyer ever since.

"Why," I ask his wife, "did he start working on the case in the first place, if he knew he would be putting his life in danger?"

"He was a prosecutor, he believed in the law," she responds. The story shows how a state apparatus that is never reined in, that is allowed to torture and murder without consequence for decades, will not be inclined to change its practices until effective mechanisms of societal, parliamentary, and court control are put in place. Unpunished crimes, like those committed in Paraguay, beget new crimes.

MONROVIAN RUINS

LIBERIA, 2005

We are in a hurry. Thompson tells our chauffeur to ignore the "No Entry" sign and drive right up to the departures hall, even though the parking there is only for military vehicles. We pull up and are about to get out of the car when several police officers approach us determinedly. They shout at us, we start to discuss, the officers shout louder. We climb out to negotiate, and after a chaotic debate, I am permitted to unload my suitcase from the car, at which point an even more determined-looking officer appears and forces us to move on. Just another day at Roberts International Airport in the Liberian capital. I'm here to catch a flight back to Brussels after a week in Monrovia.

The path to the departures buildings takes us past a line of people in uniforms, and access is for passengers only. Thompson falls at the first hurdle. Julia is white, blonde, and is carrying some of my luggage; she is seen as my travel companion and is let through. At the next barrier, they want to see tickets; we claim we only have electronic versions with us. At the next gate—all of this before we get to the check-in desk and the security controls—we get caught out. I'm the only one who has a ticket. I say that Julia is my fiancée and we want to spend the last moments together before the flight, a line that works well here and at all the subsequent checks. At nearly every turn people ask for a present; I smile naively and pretend I don't understand. I check in. We want to go back out again so I can say goodbye to the people I've spent the last few days with. At each gate the negotiations begin again—ticket, presents, access denied. I tell them the security people behind us gave me permission to leave the building. Finally, I get to the outdoor waiting area to say a final goodbye to Thompson Ade-Bayor, president of Liberia Watch for Human Rights, along with Julia (Littmann) who works with the International Federation for Human Rights in Paris. All around us are police officers, security men, vendors, money changers, beggars. And all of them want something from us.

***

Along with human rights, corruption was one of the major themes of this trip in August 2005, my first visit to Africa. It all started with a call from the International Federation for Human Rights and the invitation to lead a delegation to Liberia. Wedged between other states torn by civil war—Guinea, Sierra Leone, and the Ivory Coast—Liberia was once described by the *Economist* as the worst country on earth. Every contemporary affliction you can think of is found here: massacres, torture, police violence, mass rape, severed limbs, war crimes, slave trading, prostitution, child labor, child soldiers, drug trading, arms trading, plunder of natural resources, environmental contamination, corruption. Human rights groups' reports from the long years of conflict here are filled with appalling details. But a sense of obligation, as well as curiosity, got the better of me, and I agreed to make the trip.

Our small delegation meets at the hotel in Monrovia. We are an odd group: Julia Littmann, always sporting flip-flops, always laughing; the reserved philosophy teacher and human rights defender Badíe Hima from Niger; and me, the German lawyer with no African experience. Our task is to work with Thompson Ade-Bayor and his young colleague, Bill Pyne, to compile a human rights report just before the elections in October. The report is intended to provide information to international forums on the situation in Liberia, partly with a view to the political negotiations after the elections. An interim government has been in charge since the 2003 ceasefire between the dictator Charles Taylor and the various warlord factions and seems to have fulfilled its mandate. A UN mission is tasked with maintaining the relative peace. Many of the combatants from the parties to civil war have now demobilized. The upcoming elections are the first since 1997. Those were won by the most powerful of warlords: Charles Taylor. His young supporters paraded through the streets with the slogan "He killed my ma, he killed my pa, I'll vote for him." One hundred fifty thousand people were killed in the Liberian civil wars between 1989 and 1996 and then again from 1999 to 2003. Hundreds of thousands of others fled to neighboring countries. Diamonds, wood, and other natural resources formed part of the spoils of war. Many industrial companies and plantations were the property of the state, and everyone helped themselves.

The security situation in the country is still volatile, according to Thompson and the Federation for Human Rights. As a result, our itinerary is limited to the capital, Monrovia, and even then we are told not to leave the hotel after dark. I heed these warnings; in Monrovia, I feel like I'm witnessing the apocalypse. The civil war seems far from over. The hazy weather and the constant rain dampen the mood across the city; the war-ravaged structures look surreal in the twilight. Along the banks of the Saint Paul River, water sloshes around clusters of shacks and buildings fallen into ruin. Most of the public buildings are mere skeletons; even the ministries we visit are only partially accessible. NGOs and trade unions work in backyards, in condemned buildings and little alleyways. Again and again, I see how violence flares up in interactions on the street or even in the stories we hear from the people we meet. The city is full of weapons and strewn with armed groups who for the past decade and a half have regularly used violence to obtain what they want.

We are seeking an unbiased impression of the human rights situation and want to avoid being instrumentalized, but it's hard to gauge the interests of the various political figures and officials we meet with. The UN mission staff, made up of people from all over the world, is well informed and as a result only cautiously optimistic. Its biggest task is to organize free and fair elections in a country with no functioning infrastructure outside the capital city, and even there it's not guaranteed. Pictures of two of the front-running candidates can be seen all around town: here the former World Bank staffer Ellen Johnson Sirleaf, supported by the West and who will go on to become Africa's first female head of state a few months after our visit; there the former international footballer George Weah, youth idol and thus favored by many demobilized soldiers.

I develop great admiration for the human rights activists that we meet. Many small organizations were set up soon after the end of the civil war with international funding. Many of them are women's groups; all work under difficult circumstances. The office of Liberia Watch for Human Rights, the group that is helping to organize our trip, is located in a small, muddy alleyway filled with garbage. The young staff is excited about our visit; we take a group picture together. The other organizations' offices are even smaller; some aren't even furnished. In spite of all this, we find an astonishing willingness to tackle the massive problems facing the country. The Ministry of the Interior is housed in a ruin close to the river. We make our way gingerly through the bullet-ridden stairwells. Two rooms have been set up as makeshift offices. It's not much better at the Justice Ministry. The minister of information seems nice and open. We meet his vice minister later on the street in front of the ministry, and we chat about his personal future. Interior Minister Dan Morias is almost jovial in conversation. Only later do we discover that as a local official he is alleged to have been responsible for one of the most terrible massacres of the war.

Liberian chief justice Henry Cooper is the third highest office holder in the state. He has a residence in the Temple of Justice where his court sits, a building that survived the war unscathed. It has a decent foyer, a conference room and a spacious, temperature-controlled office for Cooper. Four members of the Supreme Court are discussing a case on his couch, and they will interrupt their meeting only very briefly on account of our visit, Cooper stresses. He is said to be one of the most corrupt people in the whole country. He doesn't have to meet with us, and he makes sure we know it. I ask a few questions and receive some throwaway responses. Corruption, the lack of courts in rural areas, high levels of pre-trial detention, long delays before trial—all of this is not his fault, I'm told, and am advised to ask the minister of justice instead.

Kabineh Janneh was a corporate lawyer before the war; now he is the interim government's minister of justice. He's the only one we meet with who offers us some tea. We talk about one of the biggest problems facing Liberia. Rape of women or girls was widespread during the civil war, and violence against women has increased since the war ended. The minister introduced a new bill that extends the definition of rape beyond sexual penetration. He also wants to ensure that suspects are not immediately released on bail so that victims don't have to encounter them again the next day. This is especially problematic in small villages, where the suspect may be the local teacher, policeman, or other authority figure. Janneh is also working to bring about constitutional reform; he says the president has an overly dominant role. "In Liberia, even Jesus and Mohammed would have become dictators," he says. Former president Charles Taylor is supposed to be extradited to Sierra Leone to stand trial at the UN tribunal there. At this point, such a move seems inconceivable, but later, in 2012, Taylor is sentenced to fifty years in prison. Janneh seems like a reasonable man and makes a good impression on us.

A rude awakening comes later in the Royal Hotel bar. We join some English journalists at their table. Dino Mahtani, West Africa correspondent for the *Financial Times,* laughs when we tell him what we thought of the day. He relates Janneh's suspected involvement in corrupt business dealings. It's only our second day in this unknown country, and we are already confused.

***

The Royal Hotel is outside the city center, set back from the main street, a long building painted a shade of terracotta. The interior is reminiscent of Rick's Café in the film *Casablanca*, a large open space with a huge bar on the left, wooden tables on the right, the ever-occupied billiards table in the background. Every night the Lebanese manager greets us in French with a handshake, and after the second day, he calls us all *habibi*, friend. The menu of Arabic appetizers, vegetable soup, chicken, and grilled fish tastes good, even when eaten day after day. It's a nice place to relax, especially since we don't dare venture out at night. Just once we make an exception and join Bobby the driver and Bill from Liberia Watch for Human Rights at a traditional restaurant downtown, in the city's badly war-damaged center, packed with market stalls and teeming with people. They're showing the Premier League on TV, Tottenham versus Chelsea. Bobby reads out the menu for us but I struggle to understand his Pidgin English. We order fufu, a kind of dumpling made from manioc and plantains; the beers served by the good-humored waiter in a red woolly hat and a Sylvain Wiltord jersey make for a pleasant atmosphere. On Wednesdays and Saturdays, part of the restaurant is turned into a dance hall where people drink and dance all night. The women cook at huge pots in a large, cavernous back room.

In the early evening, the waiter accompanies us outside. As he says goodbye he bends down to the passenger window of the car and gives us the thumbs up. Suddenly it all kicks off: in one fluid movement he turns around and without hesitation punches the man beside him in the face, shouting, "Gimme my money back!" While he was talking to us through the window, a thief had taken money from his trouser pocket. They start to fight. A bunch of people gather around. Bobby drives us away immediately. We've now got an idea of how quickly a peaceful situation here can turn violent.

***

A few days later, I'm at the airport before my flight back. I've said goodbye to the rest of the team and am trying to make my way back to departures, this time alone, and without the usual negotiations at each turn. Some of the security staff get annoyed because I still won't pay them anything. But I get a warm "Hi Wolfgang" from Beverly at the immigration counter. On my way into the country, I'd translated my name into English for her: *the path of the wolf.*

Then a pleasant surprise: instead of the usual sterile airport café, I find a little wood-paneled bar near the waiting area. West African rhythms play from the speakers, and the bartender keeps me supplied with Liberian Club Beer. I meet David, who is also waiting for the flight to Brussels. He is a ship's captain on his way home to England on leave for his sister's wedding. He's been a seaman in West Africa for ten years. He learned to sail when he was eight and has spent nearly his whole life at sea. His wife is from Karachi; he met her in Gambia. He then followed her to New York and started working as a fitter for shipping companies. But he couldn't get used to the settled life. She moved back to Gambia, where David bought her a bar that she still runs. And now they are in process of separating. He still loves her but he's a sailor, he doesn't want to give up life at sea. During our conversation, when he says the word *she*, he generally means not his wife but his ship, an agile sixty-meter freighter that's small enough to maneuver the often tricky coastal waters of West Africa. He worked his way up from sailor to captain. At thirty-one, he's still young. He's not authoritarian toward his crew, despite the strict hierarchy at sea: he's the boss, then come the English officers, and then the local sailors.

David tells me about the tedious formalities at customs in Monrovia. Dozens of people come on board, everyone's shouting, giving orders, and everyone accepts the bribes set aside for them. Once the Liberian officials have been paid off, he and his crew spend two days working their way through Monrovia's bars: beer, schnapps, and women, exactly how a landlubber would imagine it. Monrovia, a dangerous city? No, he says, you just need to have a good sense for the place and a bit of tact.

I ask David what kinds of goods he transports. His answer is vague: oil, containers, equipment. Over the years the routes have been pushed further south, from Senegal via Gambia and Guinea-Bissau to Sierra Leone and now to Liberia again. His next destination is the border region between Liberia and the Ivory Coast. David's routes take him to places where, over the past few years, the shipping of goods has enabled wars, directly and indirectly, by helping to finance the fighting: weapons of all kinds, especially light arms like Kalashnikovs, small enough to be handled by child soldiers. Drugs, gold, diamonds, rubber, and high-grade woods. And then there's the trade in human cargo: women and refugees. Liberia is controlled by political elites so far beyond the reach of the law that they can seize control of plantations and steal timber and mineral ores for sale on the black market. Four hundred tons of latex is said to have disappeared in this way from the port of Buchanan.

There are frequent allegations surrounding the US company Firestone. This multinational corporation ran the world's biggest rubber plantation in Liberia and dominated the Liberian economy for decades, in close cooperation with Charles Taylor. Firestone once even wanted to bring in warships when the country couldn't repay its loans during the economic crisis of the 1930s. Liberia, an independent state since its foundation in 1847 by US colonial groups seeking to resettle freed slaves, has fallen into a quasi-colonial relationship with the multinational.

Firestone is also a subject of interest to Alfred Brownell, Liberia's most important human rights lawyer, whom we meet the day after our evening adventure to the restaurant. In torrential rain, we stumble endlessly through unlit houses and hallways until we finally locate him by mobile phone. Brownell shows us photos he took on his travels in rural areas: images of slave labor and pollution. Conditions on the rubber plantations are still inconceivably awful. The workers are exposed to ammonia and other poisons without any protection, and some of them go blind as a result. Entire regions become contaminated through pollution. Workers are physically abused. We see photos of disfigured bodies with huge open wounds. Every day each worker is responsible for up to 950 trees, which must be marked and cleaned before extracting the rubber. They can't do this alone, so they bring in children sometimes; some are from their own families, some are child refugees, some as young as four or five.

In one of Brownell's photos, we see Justice Minister Janneh, our friendly interview partner from the second day of our trip, along with some other ministers. They made the journey from Monrovia to the regional capital of Buchanan to personally ensure the arrest of ninety-three small landowners who had protested against the proposed use of their land by LAC, the country's second-largest rubber company after Firestone. The ministers have their own personal financial interests in the project. The protestors were locked up, first on the plantation, then in the county jail. Alfred's pictures show skinny youths and frightened-looking men behind barbed wire, in front of them an angry throng of people calling for their release, as well as Alfred and his colleagues,

who managed to get a court to order their release and then persuade the
initially reluctant police chief that he was obliged to enforce it.

Alfred Brownell studied in New Orleans and is well acquainted
with the Alien Tort Claims Act so effectively revived by Peter Weiss. He
plans to file a lawsuit in the United States in the coming months seeking compensation for the plantation workers. We discuss the possibilities for bringing European companies before European courts for their
human rights violations. It's not just the notorious blood diamonds.
Trade in other goods also helped support the wars in West Africa; several European firms had lucrative business dealings with warlords
from all parties to the conflicts.

***

On Sunday afternoon we drive to the harbor. We cross the Saint Paul River
and drive along the riverbanks, past ruins, slums, huge rubbish dumps.
The UN checkpoints lie on the other side of the water. Few people know
what it's like inside the settlements along the road leading through this
once-civil-war-ridden region, how many weapons might be stored there.
Some talk about the great success of the disarmament campaign, but any
number of former combatants are living here, including former child soldiers who have killed and tortured. How are they supposed to find their
place in the new society? In one settlement we see a white UN tank, its
cannon pointed toward a group of people for no apparent reason.

Traffic is heavy; the streets are in poor condition. Small children
patch up tires, men repair umbrellas, furniture is made and restored
in open wooden workshops at the side of the road. People wait in line
in front of a shack where a film is due to be shown. Cars are cleaned
at carwashes in pools of water along the road, in a region where
drinking water supplies are patchy at best. There are endless rows
of market stalls and mud streets leading to the nearby slums. And

people everywhere, on foot, on bikes, constantly dodging the craterous potholes and the cars swerving around them, wheelbarrows and handcarts, many stacked with long logs of timber, motorbikes, pickup trucks with people sitting and standing in the back, fuel tankers. The overcrowded yellow Nissan taxis stop every few meters, holding up the already congested traffic, to pick up more passengers. Everyone is beeping their horn, trying to push their way through. Jeeps overtake in the narrowest of spaces, careening dangerously past pedestrians on the hard shoulder, the UN jeep drivers the most aggressive of all. The people are in suits, bright shirts, and dresses, long djellabas, football jerseys—Kaká, Ronaldinho, and in one case Ballack—and baseball caps. The suffering and the effects of the war can be seen all around: people washing in muddy pools of water, beggars in rags, cripples, mothers picking lice from their children's hair.

We turn off the main road, beeping the horn to make our way through the masses of people, and pull up in front of a one-story building where the family of our young travel companion Bill lives. He's invited us to visit them. We climb out, and the family surrounds us, we shake hands and pose for photos. The neighborhood doesn't seem that dangerous.

After a while, we leave these densely populated areas behind us and drive toward the Hotel Africa, now a ruin but once a luxury hotel. Swedish and Polish UN soldiers have set up provisional camps in the hotel's shadows. Behind the building, a sandy path lined with makeshift shacks leads down to the beach. We stop at a small beach club where the friendly owner, Francis, apologizes that they've run out of fish. We sit under palm trees at a little wooden table drinking cold Club Beer, looking out onto a sandy beach that's empty apart from a few children jumping in the waves. I jog a few meters with Bobby, who is endlessly amused by how quickly I start sweating. When he was younger, Bobby played football in Liberia's top league. He takes off his shirt; much of his body is now scarred. During a skirmish in the civil war, he sought refuge in a church; the building was shelled, people died all around him, he was hit by shrapnel.

***

The grimmest part of our journey begins a few days later. We're standing in front of the Monrovia Central Prison Compound, which is surrounded by a two-meter-high barbed wire-topped wall, waiting to be let inside. A young woman in uniform knocks on the heavy steel door. An older man in uniform barks back at her until he spots us, and then opens the door. Two young UN soldiers keep watch in the pouring rain in front of small concrete barracks.

We are greeted in an austere room by the director, a man in his mid-thirties in an army-style vest and baseball cap. The state prosecutor who is accompanying us says a few stiff words of thanks to the director for letting us visit. Gesturing to a large blackboard, the director explains that there are 281 detainees today, including 7 women. The different cells are represented on the board, with the names of the detainees below. There are several names to each cell, except for one cell that has just one detainee. When we ask about it we are told he is so dangerous it took several police to arrest him. According to the board, 50 prisoners are here for murder, 40 for rape, and another 40 for robbery. The director explains that unfortunately there aren't enough beds and mattresses for all the inmates. I've gotten to know prisons in Belarus, Turkey, Spain, France, and Germany and I know that questions about prison conditions are generally met with whitewashed answers. We decide to ask them anyway. The director assures us that there are no children imprisoned, apart from one sixteen-year-old accused of murder. He says that, yes, most of the prisoners are in pre-trial detention, and yes, some of them have to wait for months before trial.

We move to the cellblocks, the rain still pouring down. Long before we get there, inmates start calling out to us from a crumbling one-story cement building, their hands stretched out through the small barred windows. Some scream and howl, others shout "no food, no food." We enter the block for serious offenders, a dark, wet cave with an infernal smell of urine and other bodily emissions. We pass by several cells with floor to ceiling bars that allow us to look in. At first, we can see very little, but then our eyes adjust. We glimpse people lying and crouching in the cells. We feel like visitors at a zoo. The inmates start to call out when they see us. We hesitate, not wanting to stop in front of any one cell, and keep moving swiftly through. None of us says anything. The director leads the way.

We turn a corner into the next wing. Suddenly we're alone; the director and the prosecutor have stayed behind, waiting to see how we react. We realize that the cells are open. We take a few steps further in and are soon surrounded by people. The group gets separated. The human rights campaigner from Niger, Badíe, the third member of our delegation, stays behind me and gets into a discussion. Julia goes all the way to the end of the cellblock, which makes me uneasy. I am encircled by eight or ten men in torn clothes, some of them without shirts. They are all shouting at me, some of them reach out to touch me, wanting to shake my hand. One of them pulls up his t-shirt and shows me the swelling on his lower stomach. All I want to do is get away, which fills me with shame. I look around to find the director, who is watching us impassively. It's as if he was testing how long we could bear it, when we would finally turn back.

We stay. I try to focus on individual people, but it's hard to follow what they're saying because people keep reaching out to touch me through the cell bars and everyone is talking at once. I understand certain things. "No food," some say. "Pig food," others say. They are only allowed out in the fresh air when visitors come. Visits must be no longer than five minutes, and many inmates never have any visitors because their families live in rural areas and can't afford to make the trip. Some of them want us to take note of their relatives' names and phone numbers because their families were never informed of their arrest. Nobody has a lawyer. If you don't have money, you don't get a lawyer, and thus don't have any chance to pay bail or offer bribes. Some of the detainees have been here for months waiting for their trial, others for years. They tell the stories of how they were arrested and protest their innocence. "We want justice," they call out. "Help us." They want us to see everything.

I assure them that we see what it's like, that we will write a report about it. I try to explain to them what we are doing here and while I'm talking realize that I don't really know. I'm ashamed of the suit I'm wearing, and the fact that I don't want to look at the wounds they show me. Amused by my hesitancy, they take me by the arms and haul me into another room. This one smells even worse; it houses the showers and toilets, but they don't work. They say that when they have problems, the doctor just gives them tablets that don't do anything. They tell me that one prisoner died just yesterday and nobody did anything; nobody even took care of his corpse. No money, so no proper burial. One man, badly injured in the war, hobbles in front of me and asks: "What am I supposed to do out there if I ever get out of here?"

Some of them just want to shake hands. Others ask me to look through the bars into their tiny, dark cells. Fifteen people in just a few square meters, no beds, just mats on the bare concrete floor. No personal belongings, except for some small plastic bags filled with oil and herbs that are tied to the bars—one guy got them from his family and sells them to the other inmates.

In another cell, I see young boys, between ten and fourteen years old, two or three heads shorter than me. They yell that they want to go to school. I can barely stand the heat, the screaming, the stink. I am filled with unbridled anger. The awfulness of this place far exceeds anything I have experienced before. When we leave the cellblock, we are met by the director, who has been waiting at the entrance the whole time. "Now you've seen everything. You should report back to the international community so that the conditions improve." His statement comes as a surprise; earlier he had been trying to gloss over how bad things were.

***

When I get back to Europe I talk to Julia regularly on the phone; she has stayed on for an extra week in Monrovia. She tells me a harrowing story: at a junction, she saw a mob chase and catch a suspected thief. They started pouring petrol on him and were about to set him on fire when she tried to get out of the car to intervene, but her travel companion stopped her and drove her away. On the phone we replay the scene over and over again: What would have happened if she had got out? Would we both have gotten out if we had been there together?

A few days later she tells me that she went out one night with a bunch of friendly, heavy-drinking journalists. She fell, breaking her arm, and was taken to a hospital that treated UN personnel. The emergency room was completely overcrowded, with injured people everywhere. The floor was covered in blood, and she had to throw away her shoes the following day. Julia is embarrassed because she hurt herself on a drunken night out and as a white European got treatment immediately, while others who were seriously injured had to wait for help.

Julia writes up our report for the International Federation for Human Rights. It is published, but I can't really judge if it has any impact. I'm weighed down by the feeling of helplessness in the face of this ongoing saga of exploitation and repression and notice how glad I am to get back to my legal work where, at least in some cases, I can make direct interventions.

"Do you know how to swim?" said Lo—, bending over me. "We're going to teach you. Take him to the tap!"

Together they picked up the plank to which I was still attached and carried me into the kitchen. Once there, they rested the top of the plank, where my head was, against the sink. Two or three Paras held the other end. The kitchen was lit only by a weak light from the corridor. In the gloom, I could just make out the faces of Ir—, Cha— and Captain De—, who seemed to have taken over the direction of these operations. Lo— fixed a rubber tube to the metal tap which shone just above my face. He wrapped my head in a rag, while De— said to him: "Put a wedge in his mouth." With the rag already over my face, Lo— held my nose. He tried to jam a piece of wood between my lips in such a way that I could not close my mouth or spit out the tube.

When everything was ready, he said to me: "When you want to talk, all you have to do is move your fingers." And he turned on the tap. The rag was soaked rapidly. Water flowed everywhere: in my mouth, in my nose, all over my face. But for a while I could still breathe in some small gulps of air. I tried, by contracting my throat, to take in as little water as possible and to resist suffocation by keeping air in my lungs for as long as I could. But I couldn't hold on for more than a few moments. I had the impression of drowning, and a terrible agony, that of death itself, took possession of me. In spite of myself, all the muscles of my body struggled uselessly to save me from suffocation. In spite of myself, the fingers of my two hands shook uncontrollably. "That's it! He's going to talk," said a voice.

Henri Alleg, *The Question*
Alleg is a French journalist who was imprisoned by the French
during the Algerian War. In this book, published in 1958,
he describes the practice of waterboarding.

FAIL AGAIN. FAIL BETTER.

NEW YORK, JERUSALEM, RAMALLAH, BERLIN, 2006

In summer 2005 Michael Ratner, Peter Weiss and I had decided that we would once again take up the legal fight against Rumsfeld. But then in autumn of that year, I was approached by Human Rights Watch, the well-established New York-based human rights organization. I learned that the Uzbek interior minister Zokirjon Almatov was in a German clinic in Hannover for treatment. He was suspected of torturing numerous detainees and killing hundreds of Muslim demonstrators with his security forces in the Andijan massacre in May 2005. I then met Lotte Leicht from Denmark, the European Union advocacy director and director of the Human Rights Watch Brussels office. Together we decided to put together material to file a criminal complaint against Almatov in Germany. Lotte, slightly younger than me and also a lawyer, had gained practical experience with war crimes trials following the Yugoslavian war. We believed we had found exactly the right case for Germany. The German public prosecutors clearly had jurisdiction because Almatov was on German territory. And following the Andijan massacre, the European Union had already agreed to impose personal sanctions against him.

It was a pleasure to work with my energetic colleague and her highly professional organization, which had much greater resources at their disposal for this kind of work compared to the Center for Constitutional Rights, and especially compared to European law firms and civil liberties organizations. We tracked down survivors and relatives of torture victims throughout Europe. Former UN special rapporteurs and law professors wrote expert opinions on questions such as why Almatov did not enjoy immunity even though he held the position of minister of the interior at that time. The former British ambassador to Uzbekistan, Craig Murray, provided his testimony for the case.

We rapidly prepared the submissions, but our efforts went nowhere. The German military needed the Uzbek airbase in Termez for their operations in Afghanistan. Almatov was warned by German authorities and left the country. Federal prosecutors in Karlsruhe abandoned the proceedings shortly afterward. From a legal point of view, the case was clear, and we acted together with Human Rights Watch and several renowned lawyers. Officially, no one denied the human rights violations committed by Uzbekistan. It was political reasons that prevented it from going to trial.

After the failed action against Almatov, I was particularly angry. This time it was "only" against an Uzbek and not against a powerful US politician and still we didn't get anywhere with it. With renewed determination, I started to work on the new Rumsfeld case. The Center for Constitutional Rights and I had big plans. This time we decided not to limit our complaint to Abu Ghraib and looked for other victims of US torture who were willing to take legal action or relatives of victims who were. We also decided to focus additionally on the lawyers of the US government who knowingly misinterpreted the law. They turned war prisoners into enemy combatants without any legal protection and tried to argue that torture was no longer torture. We wanted to approach the whole case more comprehensively, involve US law professors, and find witnesses from within the ranks of the US administration.

***

Ever since my first visit to the Center in New York City, I have always stayed with Michael's family in their townhouse in Greenwich Village. The house is only ten minutes away from the office. I walk right through Washington Square and pass by New York University. My workplace at the Center is right next to the office of the super, Alberto, an elderly man from Panama who plays the trumpet in his spare time and greets me as I arrive every morning. It doesn't take long to get to know all my colleagues at the Center. Many of them work on Guantánamo and torture, but discrimination against African Americans and police repression are also ever-present topics in the office. The founders of the Center were of Jewish descent. Today people from various different backgrounds work here, but you could say they are all informed by a distinctly Protestant work ethic. They eat their homemade lunches in front of their computers. They might stop for a quick coffee but otherwise work the whole day through. There is barely time for anything more than quick chats. I adapt to the office, work a lot, and still try to find some time to explore this fascinating city.

I accompany Michael to dinners, receptions, and exhibition openings where I meet wealthy funders of the Center and other solidarity initiatives. I wonder why I don't meet people like this in Germany. Is it because back home I don't have access to these sorts of circles? Or because social initiatives in the United States are often funded by private philanthropy while the government keeps out of such work? In Germany, state institutions take on a greater range of public services, but the murder of the Jews by the Nazis has extinguished an entire culture of philanthropy and civil society.

***

In April 2006 Michael and I visit the Dakota Apartments, the complex overlooking Central Park and in front of which John Lennon was shot.

Inside, Yoko Ono is waiting for us in the apartment she once shared with him. On the way there Michael tells me about how he once visited the couple in a basement apartment in the West Village while looking to drum up support for the defense of people in the militant black movement. At that time Lennon was politically active on behalf of Michael Abdul Malik, aka Michael X, a controversial Black Power activist who led a commune in Trinidad and who was executed in 1975 after being convicted of murder. Today Yoko wants to speak with Michael because the Center is set to receive the LennonOno Grant for Peace. But we wonder if she might also be interested in supporting our new project.

The seventy-three-year-old is a bundle of energy and extremely politically aware. But she gets wary when we talk about the torture cases against the United States. She is still a Japanese citizen, and though she has lived here for a long time, she still has to worry about her visa and residency status. Her experiences of surveillance and denunciation by the FBI on account of the pair's anti-war activities left her with a lasting trauma.

Later on, I get into a discussion with her. She wants to make the title of her new song—"Healing"—into a global motto. She argues that it would be very healing for us Germans to make peace with the crimes of our past. I strongly disagree, stressing how important it is to keep the memories of Nazi crimes alive, and criticizing the flawed downplaying of those horrors by some historians and politicians. We don't manage to reach any kind of agreement on the issue, and later Michael says to me with a laugh, "You won't get much support with that approach, but that's just the way you are."

A few days later I attend a peace movement talk at Columbia University. The audience is made up of the usual suspects. But one woman on the podium—mid-fifties, with a suit, harsh features, and tied-back hair—seems somewhat out of place. She is Janis Karpinski, the general who commanded a military police unit in Iraq and thus oversaw Iraqi prisons. When the Abu Ghraib photos came out, she was removed from her post.

I introduce myself as the German lawyer who brought the criminal complaint against Donald Rumsfeld and others for torture at Abu Ghraib. She smiles. "Very good," she says.

"By the way," I say, "you were one of the people we included in the complaint as suspects. We want to make a new complaint against Rumsfeld and now think we might have been wrong about you."

"Aha," she says. "Now you know better."

I ask Karpinski if she'd be prepared to have a longer conversation with me and end up visiting her a few days later at her home in a Boston suburb. When I arrive she is relaxed and informal, and I'm surprised to see that she has a rainbow flag on her balcony. A lot of time has passed since her suspension and demotion, but she is still full of anger. She maintains that she lost her job not because of misconduct, but because she's a woman and thus doesn't have the same access to power as the men.

I lay out a map of the prison complex in front of her to get firsthand knowledge of Abu Ghraib; I need names and facts. She tells me where the abuses took place. Then we talk about the responsibility of certain people, especially Geoffrey Miller, the Guantánamo commander who, on a visit to Iraq, propagated the kinds of illegal interrogation methods used at the prison in Cuba. Karpinski confirms our hypothesis that the torture practices migrated from Afghanistan in late 2001 to Guantánamo and then to Abu Ghraib and beyond. She is prepared to give testimony in Germany—a remarkable move for someone for whom the army has long been like family.

In New York, we speak to other potential witnesses. Like Janis Karpinski, Lawrence Wilkerson is a long-serving officer and was chief of staff to Secretary of State Colin Powell. Before we start talking about torture he tells us about his son, who is also in the military and who is having issues with his wife; she threatened to leave him if he accepted another call-up to Iraq as he approached the end of his service. That he speaks so candidly with us about these things, though he knows our leftist positions, is another example for me of the open culture of conversation in the United States.

He has clear words for us on other topics too: both he and Powell are full of resentment toward Vice President Cheney and Donald Rumsfeld. They feel they were manipulated when Powell was persuaded to make a plea for the Iraq war in an address to the United Nations in February 2003 based on information that later turned out to be false. Wilkerson says he is strongly opposed to torture and that he was part of a network of senior military figures who felt the same way. I try to persuade him to act as a witness in Germany or to support the case in some other way. But for him, this is going too far. It's one thing to make political statements in the United States, but supporting criminal proceedings abroad against US politicians and military figures would not go down well in military circles.

I spend months trying to make contact with some of the torture victims or their relatives. Traveling to Guantánamo wouldn't make much sense. I wouldn't be allowed to speak to the detainees. Lawyers there have to go through an extensive clearing procedure, filling out endless forms on their contacts, their political connections, even drug consumption. After all that they aren't allowed to take away their notes from meetings with detainees, but must first submit them to the Pentagon, where they are censored. This is a wholly unreasonable procedure that I'm not prepared to accept. The security situation in Iraq means we can't travel there either, so we have to rely on middlemen for witness statements and for communicating with clients. This is a very different situation from the Argentina proceedings. For those cases, we have direct contact with the victims and feel a political connection to the victims and their relatives. With many of the former detainees in Iraq or Guantánamo we don't know anything about their political positions. Some of them certainly advocate for views that we oppose. But what is incontrovertible, and what goes beyond these differences, is our unshakable belief that torture is always a crime.

Shortly before our deadline for submitting the complaint I finally get to speak with some victims on the phone with the help of an interpreter. They are remarkably open in speaking about the abuse they suffered, including sexual degradation, and about the long-term effects of torture that they all suffer from: sleep issues, difficulties concentrating. None of them are getting any kind of therapeutic care. We talk about their expectations for the case, which are aligned with ours. They are glad we are submitting a complaint, but they know that it will be difficult to overcome the political resistance. They are placing their hopes in a different America, the democratic America that includes the organizations and the lawyers that I work with.

We too are placing our hopes in this America again. One of our advisors recommended that we wait to submit the complaint after the midterm elections in November 2006, halfway through Bush's mandate, on the basis that this would bring more favorable circumstances. And it does. The Republicans lose several seats in both houses. One day later—a week before our planned submission date—Bush announces Rumsfeld's resignation as Secretary of Defense. In the immediate aftermath of this news, the media looks only at his military accomplishments and his missteps after the occupation of Iraq. But we leak then the news of our complaint and Al Jazeera, CNN, and the BBC pick it up and discuss it. We are pleased with the worldwide attention. We have managed to trigger a debate on torture and the criminal responsibility of Rumsfeld and others.

A long article about me by Jana Simon appears in the German newspaper *Die Zeit*. It's a well-written piece and I'm glad that our case has been given so many prominent column inches. In the article, I'm described as being driven and tormented by the significance of the cases as well as being unapproachable, stern, and hostile. Unsurprisingly, it doesn't exactly line up with how I see myself. What I find more problematic is the large photo of me and the headline: "The man taking on Rumsfeld." Friends tell me that I now have a more prominent role and need to live up to this new image of a human rights lawyer. I see myself as something of a driving force, yes, but just one out of many people in the United States and Germany who worked on the project for months, lawyers from the Center as well as students, trainees, and a whole host of other lawyers. And we are also representing other figures and human rights organizations. Our message should be: here is an international network mobilizing against Rumsfeld. In the end, the complaint is co-signed by dozens of human rights organizations from Latin American, Africa, and Europe, as well as prominent figures like the Nobel Peace Prize winner Adolfo Perez Esquivel.

***

It is November 14 and the day has finally come. The huge public interest in our complaint has caused our stress levels to soar over the past few days. We have been sifting through documents, expert opinions, and witness statements right until the last minute to finalize our complaint. Michael Ratner and Peter Weiss arrive in Berlin and on the night before filing there are over a dozen people in the office working on the submission. At six in the morning, we email the Federal Public Prosecutor in Karlsruhe, attaching the 383-page criminal complaint that more than a dozen of us have been working on for over a year.

The most interesting case included in the complaint concerns Saudi Arabian citizen Mohammed al-Qahtani, who is suspected of being involved in the September 11 attacks. He was arrested in Afghanistan in autumn

2001 and has been held in Guantánamo since 2002. Despite the extensive limitations on communication at Guantánamo, he joined our complaint through his lawyer. He wants to draw attention to his story and hopes for compensation. Studying his case reveals the well-planned and systematic implementation of an interrogation plan encompassing torture. Donald Rumsfeld was directly involved in al-Qahtani's treatment, procedures that are documented in an interrogation log that has now been published. It provides powerful evidence of the bureaucracy of torture.

Al-Qahtani was held in solitary detention for one hundred sixty days in a tiny cell with no natural light. During this time he was interrogated, sometimes for twenty hours a day, and was woken whenever he fell asleep. His guards stripped him and forced him to stand with his legs spread in front of female guards who mocked him. He was forced to wear women's underwear on his head, as well as a bra. The military officers threatened him with dogs and put him on a leash. He was told his mother was a whore. In December 2002 he underwent a fake kidnapping. He was kept in the cold. He was administered large quantities of intravenous fluids and denied access to a toilet. At one point his heart rate fell to thirty-five beats per minute, and he was hooked up to a heart monitor.

Government documents show that Rumsfeld was personally involved in these illegal practices. On December 2, 2002, he signed a memo permitting a range of interrogation tactics including hooding, stripping, the use of dogs, and what was described as "mild, non-injurious physical contact." At the bottom of the memo is the infamous handwritten note from Rumsfeld, referring to the proposal to have detainees stand in stress positions for up to four hours: "I stand for 8-10 hours a day. Why is standing limited to 4 hours?"

It's rare to see contempt for other humans displayed so clearly. Rumsfeld was well aware that forced standing and other stress positions were torture methods used by his enemies of old, the North

Vietnamese, the Chinese, and the Russians. These techniques often lead to severe health problems and can even lead to death. For decades, the United States had, in human rights reports, called these methods by their proper name: torture. In a public declaration al-Qahtani described his situation in the following words:

> A human being needs four main things in life that were taken from me at Guantánamo. First, to honor religion and freedom to practice religion and respect it. Two, honoring his personal dignity by refraining from humiliating a human being through beating or cursing him and bad treatment in general. Three, respect for his honor, which means not dishonoring him through sexual humiliation or abuse. Four, respect for human rights, by allowing a human being to sleep and be comfortable where he is; to be in a warm shelter; to have security for his life; to have sufficient food and beverage; to have means to relieve himself and clean his body; to have humane medical treatment; and to know that his family is safe from threats or harm. Again, all of these rights were taken from me.

He suffered serious physical and psychological injuries as a result of his abuse and lost nearly half of his weight. At the time of the submission of our complaint, he was suffering from post-traumatic stress syndrome, gaps in his memory, difficulties concentrating, and anxieties. He refused to be treated by doctors at Guantánamo as they were involved in the interrogations.

At this point, we've been working with the Hamburg lawyer Bernd Wagner and others on an analysis of the legal work by Bush's lawyers. We've had many long debates with him on whether we could stretch the criminal law that far and hold lawyers accountable for the actions of their "clients." The government lawyer John Yoo and other legal advisors drafted the "torture memos," which purport to justify exceptions to the ban on torture and seek to redefine what qualifies as torture. In doing so they paved the way for Rumsfeld to do what he did. Generally speaking, lawyers are not held criminally liable for their legal advice, but in this case we are all agreed: John Yoo and others crossed a line and allowed themselves to be instrumentalized to ensure the smooth organization of systemic torture. During the Nuremberg Justice Trials of 1947, the International Military Tribunal convicted Nazi lawyers and judges of the "conscious participation in a nationwide government-organized system of cruelty and injustice, in violation of the laws of war and of humanity, and perpetrated in the name of law by the authority of the Ministry of Justice, and through the instrumentality of the courts." The court found that the "dagger of the assassin was concealed beneath the robe of the jurist." We think the lawyers of the Bush administration played a similar role.

After we submit the complaint to the prosecutors in Karlsruhe, I go home to have breakfast and get changed. Later that day I join Peter, Michael, and others for a public presentation of our campaign at a big event in Kino Babylon, a historical cinema in central Berlin. Jannis Karpinski has also traveled from the United States to attend. It's a significant day for me. Hundreds of people have turned up, including many German and international lawyers. We give interview after interview explaining the background of our legal action. It's a delicate balancing act. We want the press coverage to help get the story out there. By submitting complaints against individuals we are making use of the drama of the criminal law, but doing so runs the risk of oversimplifying issues. We accept that some media will crave a sensational story, but try to draw attention to the broader system of torture that still needs to be fought through legal and political battles.

We still don't know if charges will ever be brought or arrest warrants issued. But we are sure about the impact of our project. An important first step has been made, and we are confident that others will be able to reap the rewards of our work, even if we do still have a long way ahead of us.

***

The international attention garnered by the case is partly due to interest in the target, Rumsfeld, but it goes beyond that. Many are interested in the fact that this is a way to challenge the powerful and to be heard. Our actions motivate others to fight human rights violations by legal means. My friend Netta Amar, a lawyer from Jerusalem, told me how, on the day we lodged the complaint, she stood up during a court hearing with our press release in her hand and declared to legal advisors from the Israeli Army: "Look at this. This is happening to Bush administration lawyers in Germany right now. Be careful what you do, or the same thing could happen to you."

In April 2007 Netta organizes a trip around Israel and Palestine and asks me to speak at some events about the Rumsfeld case and the future of universal jurisdiction. The first event is at the prestigious Hebrew University in Jerusalem. A law professor picks me up, and as we make our way across the huge campus to the lecture hall, he dissects and criticizes the German prosecutors' 2005 decision not to open investigations into Rumsfeld. Later on, we have a high-level discussion in a small group that includes a uniformed legal advisor to the Israeli Army and two government lawyers. The two lawyers provide legal advice to the Israeli state whenever there's a criminal complaint directed against the Israeli military or politicians—most recently in Belgium when Ariel Sharon was charged in connection with the 1982 massacre at the Palestinian refugee camps Sabra and Shatila. A surprisingly open conversation ensues—probably due to the fact that my work concerns the United States and not Israel.

In Ramallah, I visit Al-Haq, one of the oldest human rights organizations in the Middle East, and give a talk in a church on criminal liability for torture. Afterward, a series of middle-aged men file past me and shake my hand. I ask about them and it turns out they are Palestinian policemen. This annoys me—if I had known they were here I would have talked about the situation in Ramallah, citing the regular reports of torture concerning the Palestinian Authority.

There's a young and engaged audience at another event at Al-Quds University in the Arab side of Jerusalem. The students focus on the human rights violations in Palestine and are skeptical as to whether the principle of universal jurisdiction can really help to change their situation. I argue that we are making a start, creating a precedent, that there will be setbacks, but that small steps in the right direction are important. But the students are impatient; they have experienced too much, every day they and their families face the reality of life under occupation. I get a better sense of the patchwork that is the West Bank while traveling north with some people from Al-Haq to a talk at the Arab American University of Jenin. The driver takes back roads to avoid some of the Israeli Army checkpoints, but we still encounter them every few kilometers, getting stuck in long lines of traffic, waiting to pass inspections. In Jenin, the walls around town have been sprayed with radical slogans, and at the university nearly all the women wear headscarves. It turns out to be another interesting discussion on the role of the law in armed conflict. The students remain skeptical.

***

In spring 2007 our second attempt to initiate investigatory proceedings against Donald Rumsfeld and others ends in failure. The German prosecutors see no link to Germany and consider it difficult, if not impossible, to investigate US state crimes in Germany. They do not accept our central argument that public prosecutors of different countries have to work collaboratively when it comes to complex international crimes. We are more convinced than ever: in order to make any progress there needs to be a way to gather evidence in one place, link it up with an investigation in a different place, and then bring charges, potentially even in a third jurisdiction. One action builds upon another; you have to start at some single point, even if for now it may not be possible to follow through with the case all the way to the end. When the Pinochet case was filed, no one could have foreseen that the ex-dictator would travel to the United Kingdom in a private capacity two years later. But the reason the arrest warrant could be issued at the right moment was that when he arrived in Europe, the groundwork had been laid, there was already substantial documentation and witness testimony concerning his crimes.

In spite of the renewed disappointment—we had worked on the project for two years—I don't doubt that it was the right thing to do. Since speaking with Ellen Marx in Argentina, I have let go of the idea that our actions need to be successful in the short term.

We continue our work on the Rumsfeld cases and push the French public prosecutor to issue an arrest warrant against the former secretary of defense during his visit to Paris in 2007, but we have no luck. We plan a criminal complaint in Spain aimed in part at highlighting the importance of the legal battle against torture. We want to demonstrate how vital it is to hold powerful actors liable for their actions. These ideas start to spread. Our project is received with great interest in other places where similar human rights violations have occurred.

At this point, I am still a partner at our law firm, but it is clear that over the years I have become increasingly removed from this work. As much as I love being a criminal defense lawyer, I cannot imagine doing only this. My travels and the cases that arise from them have expanded my horizons and the dimensions of my legal work. Recently the everyday lawyering—the almost daily court hearings, the meetings and briefs to be written—have seemed ever less satisfying. Though important, all of these are standalone, unrelated cases. Defending individuals, especially the poor and the politically active, against the state's sometimes overly vigorous powers of prosecution is, of course, a form of human rights work. This is the conviction I have held since I started out as a defense lawyer. But more and more I see a broader picture with more complex problems. I want to participate in something that goes beyond the individual case. I want to be part of a political project.

In the November days after filing the big Rumsfeld complaint, we have a long-overdue debate at our law firm in Berlin. Some of my colleagues are complaining that I have overstretched the resources of the office with the project. They say I've been relying on those earning the money with their day-to-day work at the courts to facilitate my work. I feel somewhat unfairly treated after all the efforts and the significant resonance of our complaint. But they have a point. The law firm is not the right forum for this kind of work. In New York, at the Center for Constitutional Rights and the American Civil Liberties Union, I have seen how it can be done. Civil liberties organizations like these are funded by donations from foundations, allowing them to work on complex projects over a long period of time in a way that a law firm could not afford to. Even if law firms like ours do take on politically motivated cases, economic logic naturally sets limits.

A few days later I discuss this with Michael Ratner while out on a walk around Kreuzberg. We look back on what we have achieved together. I realize that I am not ready to let go of this kind of political work. Michael encourages me. Slowly an idea starts to form; it might be time for me to embark on something new.

This suggestion comes not from Michael but from another friend, the sociologist Erwin Single. I wonder if I shouldn't take a break for a longer period to travel and maybe work on a PhD. But he stresses that we need to take advantage of the momentum from the Rumsfeld complaint. After our conversations my mind is made up: I want to set up a new, financially independent organization that can take legal actions to defend human rights around the world, like the Center for Constitutional Rights has been doing for decades in New York.

I get to work, full of energy. We are a small bunch at first: Erwin Single, my young colleague Miriam Saage-Maaß, and me. Together we make plans, write concept notes, and look into potential funding options since at this stage there is no money. Then I take a step that many of my colleagues cannot understand: I hand in my notice at the law firm and step down as chairman of the Republikanischer Anwaltsverein. One of the other board members asks me where the money for the new project is going to come from. When I tell him that I don't know yet but that I'm confident, the board members give me telling looks. A typically German reaction, I think. I leave a successful law firm to start something new, to follow an idea that has yet to be fully finalized; most people cannot understand this. Any support I get for the move comes mainly from the more open, less risk-averse people on the other side of the Atlantic. People in the United States prove more comfortable with the idea of making a new start than my German friends.

A few months later, in spring 2007, I am sitting with a small group of German and European lawyers, including Lotte Leicht and Michael Ratner, in our law firm in Prenzlauer Berg, Berlin. They encourage me to set up an organization that is not just German but also European. It's true that the kind of work we are planning doesn't make any sense if it is limited to the national level. Our opponents—whether it's the CIA or multinational corporations—are operating across borders. We have to be organized in the same way.

***

On March 5, 2007, we set up a new non-profit organization in Berlin: The European Center for Constitutional and Human Rights—ECCHR. I start to approach foundations and private sponsors in Berlin, London, and New York. It proves to be difficult, especially in the beginning. Some potential funders are interested in the new project, but at the time of my departure from the law firm in 2008, ECCHR does not have any funds. And so the organization starts its work in a small, dark office in Prenzlauer Berg, living hand to mouth. Then, on top of everything, the foundation we placed most of our hopes on loses all of its money in a financial scandal linked to the Bernie Madoff fraud case. My days are taken up with endless practical and organizational problems that seem to have nothing to do with human rights. At dinner one night my colleagues from the law firm laugh at me: Now Wolfgang, the one who always tried to dodge it, is having to deal with mountains of admin work.

During this time it is the experiences gained in the Argentinean and the Rumsfeld cases that encourage me and give me the energy to continue. We didn't have many resources then either, but in some respects, we managed to have a lot of political and legal impact. With ECCHR we want to bring human rights violations before the European courts, no matter where they are committed, with the Pinochet case as our model. As in that case, we see that the impetus for legal action often comes from the people affected by the crimes who are fighting for their rights in their home countries. How can those of us in Europe support the fight against ongoing impunity and denial of rights elsewhere? How can we use international and regional mechanisms to overcome legal obstacles in cases where all local remedies are exhausted? And there is something else that's important for us: we want to use legal means to address the role played by European corporations in human rights violations. This is a new project and one that proves even more difficult than the task—already challenging enough—of bringing torturers and war criminals before the courts.

***

We have a long road ahead, that much is clear to me right at the beginning when I present the concept of ECCHR in Lima in spring 2008. The EU-Latin America summit is being held there, and some regional and international globalization critics have organized a counter-summit. The response to my presentation is encouraging. It's not a bad idea, they say, to file lawsuits from Europe in cases of the torture and murder of trade unionists or of environmental activists, but by that point, it's really too late for an intervention to avert the harm. What could we do, they ask, against a mining company, for instance, that is poisoning the ground and the water in Peru? I launch into a long-winded explanation of how international criminal law is more about crimes directed against people. I say that economic and social human rights like the right to water or to adequate housing are a lot more difficult to enforce and that environmental pollution falls under the remit of national courts. The audience nods along, but I can see that they are not convinced by the potential of international law and of organizations like ours. I have to accept this. I recognize that our project is a work in progress, and that if we want to achieve anything we are going to have to focus a lot more on the perspective of those affected by rights violations and not get overly caught up in a concept we devised in Berlin.

This also means that we cannot simply sit in our Berlin office and wait for cases to land on our doorstep. In October 2008 we invite three dozen lawyers from around the world to a business and human rights workshop in Berlin to discuss their experiences filing lawsuits against corporations. While moderating one discussion, I notice something odd about the way the audience is seated. My colleagues from

Europe and the United States are all together on my left, and the lawyers from the Global South, from Congo, Chad, Cameroon, Colombia, and the Philippines on my right. During one of those hermetic discussions about legal details, one of my colleagues from the right side, Colin Gonsalves, founder of the influential Human Rights Law Network (HRLN), starts to speak. "It's good to know that there is a European Center and all these networks that are ready to support us with lawsuits in Europe. But we also want you to join us in our countries. We want you to participate in our local actions as well. You should visit us and discuss strategies with those affected on the ground."

In this moment I see that our initial hypothesis falls short. We are acting like a regular law firm, just one specializing in human rights. We are waiting around in Berlin for the cases to reach us through colleagues, networks, and people affected by crimes. But Colin is asking more from us. We need to understand what's happening in countries like India, and we need to work more proactively and strategically with organizations like his and before deciding what would be our most useful contribution. We need to discuss strategy with affected people and communities and on that basis decide whether to launch actions in Delhi, Berlin, Rome, or in several places at once.

There is no shortage of ideas or inspiration, but it will take years before they manifest themselves in concrete projects. I saw this with the Argentina cases that we started to work on almost ten years earlier. It took time, but now hundreds of cases are pending before domestic courts there. That is partly why I still travel to Argentina, to follow up on the current developments; too often human rights work focuses on short-term cases instead of considering the wider picture. Where necessary and desired, we are happy to help out and get involved in the Argentine proceedings. But for me, it is not just work that brings me to the Rio de la Plata every year. That's a place where I feel at home and where I am always happy to reunite with old friends.

VICTORIES IN THE FIGHT AGAINST IMPUNITY

BUENOS AIRES AND JUJUY, 2008

I am headed toward the provincial town of San Miguel, an hour from Buenos Aires, to visit Ellen Marx. She has moved to a retirement complex named after the Jewish philanthropist Alfredo Hirsch. It's surrounded by parklands and close to the childcare center where she worked for over fifty years. The city had become too much for her, so now she lives here in a small, ground-floor apartment. When we go for a walk, I notice that her stoop has become more pronounced. She tells me about the flowers that grow nearby and seems to be happy to live amongst nature. She has found her peace in San Miguel.

Throughout her life, Ellen took care of others, and she continues to do so. A list of activities offered by the retirement home is pinned to the wall in the foyer, groups about German literature and German music—most of the Jewish people living here were born in Germany. Ellen is in charge of the library, taking care of those who use it and those who are no longer reading. She pulls me aside and whispers in conspiratorial tones. "Look, see that older gentleman over there?" she says, herself almost eighty-six years old. "He was feeling low and didn't want to read anymore, but I didn't give up and kept leaving books out for him until I figured out that he likes comedy." An even older lady is sitting on a chair at the edge of the lawn. Ellen tells me that the woman is a survivor of the Warsaw Ghetto Uprising and that Ellen is going to write her story for the newsletter published by the home.

We go to the canteen. The residents sit at big tables where women in white smocks serve food. "*En castellano!*" one of them shouts; many of the old people are hard of hearing. They are supposed to speak Spanish, but a lot of the people converse only in German, the language of their childhoods. The food is miserable, the air is sticky, I feel like fleeing from the place. I get pangs of conscience: can't people—can't we—offer anything better to these people, so many of whom are refugees?

We drink coffee in Ellen's small flat. She still collects newspaper clippings. "Look," she says, "couldn't we do something with this?" But it's not like it was before. She is not like she was before.

***

The proceedings we initiated in Germany are now almost at an end. The prosecutors in Nuremberg have closed the German-Jewish cases on the basis that the kidnapped children of our Jewish clients are Argentineans and not Germans, so there's no jurisdiction. They also argue that in the cases of the disappeared it will not be possible to prove murder as set out under German criminal law since nobody knows what actually happened to the victims. It's a rationale that goes against all historical findings and that is extremely difficult to explain to our Argentine friends. The Mercedes case is closed in reliance on the same argument. I had been particularly annoyed to see that the witness testimony from torture survivor and trade unionist Héctor Ratto, a man I had come to admire greatly, was deemed to be not credible and dismissed.

And yet we have achieved a lot, the German Coalition Against Impunity together with the victims' relatives group. The prosecution authorities in Nuremberg-Fürth have investigated around fifty cases since 1998, the biggest investigation into extraterritorial crimes since the cases relating to war crimes in the former Yugoslavia. Two of our best-known cases concern the German citizens Klaus Zieschank and Elisabeth Käsemann; these cases were different because, unlike many others, their bodies were found during the dictatorship period. In November 2003 the Nuremberg district court issued arrest warrants against the former Junta heads Jorge Rafael Videla and Emilio Eduardo Massera in connection with the deaths of Zeischank and Käsemann, and in 2004 the German government sent extradition requests. These developments in Germany, along with other trials and convictions in absentia in Italy and France, and almost a hundred arrest warrants against members of the Argentine military issued by Judge Baltasar Garzón and others in Spain, all helped to step up the pressure initially brought about predominantly by the human rights movement in Argentina.

In 2003 the newly elected president of Argentina, Néstor Kirchner, decided to repeal the amnesty laws while, at the same time, granting additional resources to the prosecutors and courts to reopen proceedings. This work is carried on by his wife and successor, Cristina Kirchner. The fact that Néstor Kirchner made the work of addressing the crimes a governmental priority in Argentina was certainly crucial for the legal success of the cases. But that wasn't the only factor. The end of impunity would have been inconceivable without constant pressure from the human rights movement, which managed to keep the issue on the agenda for over thirty years.

There are several hundred investigations ongoing across Argentina when I visit Ellen in San Miguel. I fill her in on how things are going, but I notice that she isn't as alert as she once was. She has gotten old, and many of the mothers of the disappeared are long dead. They didn't get to see their long decades of political work bearing fruit. The group of German relatives doesn't meet anymore, either. They do run into one another now and then at the German embassy, which for many years now has been inviting them to their events. They are happy to get the invitations despite the bad experiences with that institution in the past, especially the lack of will to act on behalf of the families of the disappeared. Ellen Marx is proud that after consulting with her and others, the embassy installed a placard in the residency's garden commemorating the disappeared, specifically—and this is particularly important to her—all thirty thousand disappeared.

On September 11, 2008, I'm at London Heathrow waiting for a flight when I get a call from an old friend of Ellen's. Ellen has had a heart attack and is in the hospital. Even though she is eighty-seven years old, I'm shocked, and briefly consider flying to Argentina. But a short while later I get another call informing me that she has died and will be buried the next day in accordance with Jewish tradition.

One of the most important people in my life is dead. I was very much influenced by Ellen's attitude—stubborn, pragmatic, never seeking the limelight. Since I met her and the other mothers, I rarely have any doubts about the significance of our work. Ellen's death came too quickly. Like all her other Berlin friends, I'm glad to be able to attend a ceremony in her honor a year later in a Jewish center in the Fasanenstraße, not far from where Ellen had lived seventy years before, surviving the pogrom known as Kristallnacht in November 1938.

***

It's a pity that Ellen and many other mothers of the disappeared are not around now to see history being made in Argentina. On December 11, 2009, the trial begins in Buenos Aires of two dozen senior officers for crimes committed at the torture center at ESMA. Among the accused are men who subjected Adriana Marcus and Betina Ehrenhaus to so much misery. I know the faces and the stories of those being led into the packed courtroom, partly from Adriana's descriptions: Jorge Acosta, the "Tiger;" Alfredo Astiz, the "Blond Angel of Death;" and Miguel

Cavallo. This hearing is the last step in a long process that we have been a part of for so many years; it's the result of a huge amount of preparatory work. After 1990, when the newly reunited German state sought to investigate crimes in the former East, they set up a special prosecution authority with several thousand staff working on the cases for many years. Here in Argentina, it was just a dozen investigators researching these old crimes. Once again it shows the importance of the decades of patience and perseverance on the part of the human rights organizations, which are now in a position to assist with the criminal proceedings by sharing the results of their own investigations.

My friends in Argentina are pleased about the reopening of the proceedings. They have never been able to forget what happened back then. But now many are reluctant to find the time and the energy to engage with the past. The journalist and author Horacio Verbitsky makes the point during one of our conversations: "I have spent decades of my life writing about this, now it's time for other, younger ones to do it." This is understandable, and it's also a smart political strategy. The trials are being monitored by members of the HIJOS—the organization of children of the disappeared. Many of the lawyers and journalists working on the cases are young. The work of addressing the crimes of the dictatorship has now passed to the next generation.

It takes me a while to figure out how I feel about it. For ten years I have worked to ensure that these trials take place. I have made this story my own, as far as such a thing is possible. Now that the language of violence has been silenced, it is time for the language of law. Here in Argentina, I'm witness to an exemplary model of criminal prosecutions. And yet I take no joy in seeing the old men being brought into the courtroom in handcuffs. It was never a sense of hatred of individuals that spurred me on. I find it strange to see thousands of people gathering on the big *avenida* outside the courtroom to watch live on a big screen as the verdict is delivered in another big case a few days after the ESMA trials began. The charges relate to murders committed as part of crimes against humanity. Each guilty verdict is met with applause from the crowd. They whistle shrilly when someone is acquitted. I find this hard to understand.

I get a better insight into what's happening when I start talking to some activists at a party later that day. After months of tension, the verdict comes as a great relief to many. A lot of people had to give evidence during the trial. They were nervous and felt threatened; some were the targets of explicit threats. The young helped the old to prepare their statements and accompanied them to the court. The court hallways were filled with tears, joy, and pain. This drama stretched on for many months and finally came to an end with the verdict. And, importantly, they told their stories and they were believed. The legal system that had been so hostile to them in earlier times had now rejected the excuses and justifications put forward by the military and their defense team and had seen fit to jail once powerful figures. It was all these emotions that started to spill out on the streets when the verdict was handed down.

Sometimes I wish that the wider public outside Argentina would pay more attention to the legal proceedings and campaigns underway there. Reporting is generally very superficial, announcing the verdicts in various trials as they are handed down. But the process of a society coming to terms with past grave crimes is not something that can be portrayed in a brief news report; the story is about more than just success or defeat in any given court case. What happened in Argentina shows that it can take decades before efforts toward justice bear fruit. You sometimes hear armchair strategists argue that in light of new global threats, we need to be able to use torture in some cases and that we shouldn't spend too much time going after those who have tortured in the past. Anyone who makes these kinds of arguments has no idea of the suffering caused by torture, and not just for the affected person itself. Their children, parents, and siblings also have to struggle with the consequences for the rest of their lives.

This is something often brought home to me by my friend Mariana Corral, the young artist whose father's disappearance has greatly shaped her artistic path. The trauma of the disappearance has impacted her entire life in ways that can be difficult for others to imagine. In small art shows, she exhibits the letter from her father in which he explains his political motives to her, already foreseeing his own fate. And she continues looking for traces of him, partly in an effort to find her own way in life. She has tracked down people who knew him and learned that in 1978 he was arrested near the border between Argentina, Brazil, and Paraguay. She speaks to friends of his across the country, all of whom recall a man who was always traveling, who never found one place to call home or knew what he wanted to do with his life. Mariana takes this uncertainty on board, learns to live with it. When she was younger she idealized her father; it gave her something to hold on to. But today she rejects the kind of leftist hero-worshipping engaged in by other children of the disappeared. It seems that what she most admires about him is not his militancy but his ability to constantly transform himself. While she doesn't say it explicitly, the fact that she will never find out what happened to her father is a constant burden for her.

Mariana is trying to close this chapter in her life and begin a new one. She covers a photo of her father in honey and caramel, places it in a box and goes to the cemetery with some friends. The Las Flores cemetery is mostly visited by Bolivian immigrants, the Aymara people, who come to honor their dead with food and music. Here Mariana buries her disappeared father.

***

While the court cases attracted a lot of attention in Buenos Aires, it's quite a different story just two hours away by plane from the capital at the foot of the Andes, near the border with Chile and Bolivia. Here, in northern Argentina, the cycle of exploitation and repression has persisted from the time of the Spanish colonialists, when the Camino Real trade route between Buenos Aires and Lima ran through the provinces Tucumán and Jujuy, to the early nineteenth century after Argentina's independence was secured in Tucumán, and later during the military dictatorship of the last century. More recently, during the economic crisis of 2001 and 2002, many poverty-stricken children died of malnutrition and related diseases—a phenomenon that was widely reported. "The people here," one human rights activist tells me, "have learned to endure, sometimes with loud protest and sometimes quietly."

When I visit Jujuy in March 2011, very little has been done to address the crimes of the past. Not a single trial has taken place, not even against the military or the police. I have come to the province to submit a legal opinion on behalf of ECCHR, setting out why, under international criminal law, there is a duty to investigate the complicity of corporations in crimes against humanity. It's a well-established legal position that the local prosecutors are failing to apply.

Specifically, it concerns the agribusiness company Ledesma which worked closely with the military dictatorship and owns large parts of the province and the city of Libertador General San Martin. On the evening of July 20, 1976, Ledesma shut down one of its power stations that supplied electricity to the whole region. Under the cover of darkness, military and police units used Ledesma vans to arrest hundreds of trade unionists and oppositionists within a radius of fifty kilometers. It's rare for company management to be so blatant about their complicity in repression. The most prominent victim was Luis Arédez, a doctor who on several occasions drew attention to the health problems suffered by sugar cane workers. His wife, Olga, rose to national prominence as a human rights activist after his disappearance. She died in 2005 from lung cancer, likely triggered by residues from the sugar cane, the very danger her husband had warned of.

There is a lot of evidence against Ledesma, but the authorities are conservative and are approaching the case very tentatively. I hope that my presence in the area will help the local human rights activists, and to this end, I take part in a public debate where for the first time the province's lawyers' guild publicly addresses the crimes of the dictatorship.

The judge meets our group—a number of torture survivors who are involved in the case, the local lawyers, and me—for the handover of our submission. Outside the building trade unionists and human rights activists stage a protest. They are only a small group that makes the assembled police officers, who are decked out in bulletproof vests and batons, seem over-the-top.

One of the demonstrators is Eva Arroyo, a small, black-haired woman who is filled with energy. Dressed in a tracksuit, she pays little attention to appearances or to what others think. Words flow out of her, an endless torrent of explanations, jokes, political statements, and questions to me. Her father, Juan Carlos Arroyo, was a political cadre in the revolutionary left movement. In 1976 he was on the run in Buenos Aires when some regime henchmen captured him and brought him to a torture camp where he was later murdered. Her mother was also at risk, so the family lived in exile in Bolivia during the years of the dictatorship. Eva was seven when she lost her father, but the full impact of what had happened didn't become real to her until 2009 when she was shown her father's bones that had been found in a mass grave. She went into shock and did not speak to anybody for almost a year.

I am received in the same court chambers when I return one and a half years later in December 2012, but this time the meeting is very different. The Kirchner government has replaced the old judge, a relic of times past, with a younger one. This judge and his small team are eager to get things done. While the crimes occurred decades ago, new leads emerge because investigations are finally being pursued with some vigor. Victims who had never given evidence before provide new information that can be linked up with what's already known. Hitherto unknown cases of disappearances are uncovered. Once again I am reminded of how important this work can be, even after so many years.

This is reinforced by another case that we are assisting with in Jujuy. The case is against the mining company Minas Aguilar, which, in the wake of the military putsch, had all unionized miners arrested. They were forbidden from going back to their jobs. I speak to one of the trade unionists from this time. He tells me that the miners and their families all lived side by side in company-owned housing. After the arrests, they were put out on the streets. Until now, no one had looked into their case or taken statements from them. They are glad that proceedings are now underway, and not just because they might finally see justice done. The case has also brought them together again as a group. Their community had been destroyed by the arrests and displacement—now they meet regularly and talk about their experiences.

While some of the political obstacles have fallen away, the victims still have a long and difficult path ahead. The company is mounting a strong defense of its managers who stand accused of crimes with advertising campaigns in the newspapers and the hiring of expensive defense lawyers, far outnumbering the inexperienced lawyers representing the victims. They also have time on their side. They are using every procedural mechanism they can find to delay the proceedings. The survivors feel helpless. They are frustrated at being denied the chance to finally appear in court and tell their stories. It shows how important the public drama of the courtroom can be for survivors and for society as a whole.

Corporations acting as accomplices to dictatorship—it's a topic that I will continue to work on, and not only in Argentina. In 2010 my artist friend Eduardo Molinari creates an exhibition at the Haus der Kulturen der Welt; it is a grim portrayal of this kind of corporate collaboration. It depicts children who were deployed to stand in fields as boundary markers for the pilots of airplanes spreading weed killer, which has highly damaging effects on the health of the affected. The title of the exhibition is The Potosí Principle. Potosí is a city in Bolivia that was once rich in silver. From the sixteenth to nineteenth centuries, mining there created great fortunes for the Spanish colonizers, their wealth obtained on the back of native Indian forced labor.

While artists are able to draw these kinds of historical connections in their work, as lawyers our reach is more limited. In our legal submissions, we can't look back too far in the past or we'll be reproached for going off-topic. Often we can only take legal action on individual cases, the outlying excesses, removed from their systemic and historical context. Keen to break out of these constraints, we seek out a dialogue with victims and social movements from the South.

We became aware of the existence of a right to have rights (and that means to live in a framework where one is judged by one's actions and opinions) and a right to belong to some kind of organized community, only when millions of people emerged who had lost and could not regain these rights. . .

Hannah Arendt, *The Origins of Totalitarianism*

FORGING NEW PATHS

BOGOTÁ, DELHI, BEIJING, 2010–2013

The trips to Argentina and other Latin American countries, as well as later visits to North America, helped to prepare me for the work ahead. We start making plans at the newly formed ECCHR. We want to expand the substantive scope of our work and turn our attention to economic actors. We want to act globally, not just in the Americas, to use legal and political instruments and strategies and work with young lawyers and with emerging groups from the Global South. These are lofty aspirations that we develop over the first few years of the organization's existence. It's slow going though. It takes several years for us to secure enough funding to leave our cramped office and move into a factory loft in Kreuzberg, Berlin where we can build a proper infrastructure.

Our approach of using a variety of legal tools to address certain issues and regions is known as strategic litigation. The concept is an Anglo-American one, largely unknown in Germany and the rest of mainland Europe, where lawyers work to win cases in the here and now, and rarely in pursuit of broader political aspirations. There is little experience in Europe with the enforcement of economic, social, and cultural rights. We have limited resources and can't pursue legal action against all the state and economic actors that might merit investigation. We continually have to make decisions on what to focus on, whether we should only work on regions that we know well, like Latin America, or whether we should go beyond the work on torture and war crimes and also look at arms dealing and corruption. Then there are practical issues like financing, cooperation with local partners, and access to evidence that will stand up in court.

We focus mainly on the liability of Western actors, who so often invoke and instrumentalize human rights to legitimize wars like the one in Afghanistan. We submit a criminal complaint against the German colonel Georg Klein, who ordered the bombing of a group of people near Kunduz, Afghanistan on September 4, 2009—the deadliest German military action since the Second World War—but the case is blocked by federal prosecutors. In summer 2008 prosecutors in Austria refuse to investigate the liability of Chechen president Ramzan Kadyrov for war crimes and torture after we presented evidence that he was planning to travel to Vienna to attend European Championship football matches. We still rely mainly on criminal law mechanisms, partly because the procedural costs are relatively affordable compared to civil lawsuits. We also make submissions to UN institutions and governments. We don't believe that we can change the world through legal action alone. The injustices we fight are often part of a broader system: a globalized economy that in many cases fails to secure even basic living conditions for those at the bottom of society. We break new legal ground by taking on cases like the factory fire in Karachi, Pakistan, and the collapse of the Rana Plaza building in Bangladesh—cases where hundreds of workers died due to the devastating state of the buildings and the insufficient security and emergency measures. It's the first time that workers in these countries have joined with organizations and lawyers overseas to bring claims before foreign courts. But even if we win these difficult cases and secure judgments against individual unscrupulous factory owners or companies, little will change for most of the workers, in the short term at least. Conscious of this, we see our work more as political and legal interventions which will sometimes bear fruit only further down the road. Fundamental improvements will require radical political and economic change. To achieve this, we need new kinds of law and legal practices. Until now the law—especially commercial, trade, and property law—has generally served as a tool of the powerful. At the same time, this is the law with which we have to work. In situations of limited statehood or repressive regimes, even a flawed legal system can sometimes offer protection against unbridled might. When conflicts are expressed in the language of law rather than the language of violence, that is already a good start. With this in mind, we set to work in Colombia.

***

Luciano Romero was the head of a food industry trade union in Colombia. After working for many years at a Nestlé factory, he was fired because of his union involvement. He received death threats and, after getting no protection from either the state or the company, was stabbed to death by paramilitaries in 2005. His story has played out many times in Colombia, but his death is well documented and is one of the few such cases that came before the courts. The judge convicted the men who murdered Romero and directed the authorities to also investigate the role played by Nestlé. Soon afterward the judge was forced into exile, and his order went unheeded.

At this point, we at ECCHR decide to take legal action against Nestlé in Europe. In September 2010 we all meet up in an old convent in the south of Bogotá to discuss the case: the Colombian lawyers representing Romero's widow, trade unionist Javier Correa, a lawyer from the Center for Constitutional Rights in New York, and Alirio Uribe from the Colombian lawyers' collective CAJAR. All of the Colombians face threats on an ongoing basis. They never go anywhere without drivers and bodyguards. Alirio is particularly nervous because there are rumors from the military that his organization may soon be the target of a bomb attack.

Our discussion is held as part of a bigger gathering of human rights lawyers from all over Latin America. We talk to them about potential legal mechanisms to challenge transnational corporations involved in human rights violations, as in the case of the Mercedes-Benz trade unionist murdered in Argentina in the seventies or in the Nestlé case— two examples of the continuity of trade unionist persecution. But we also discuss mining projects in Argentina and Peru, allegations against a Spanish electricity company accused of causing the deaths of several customers in Colombia through faulty power lines, and pollution from a Thyssen steelworks in Brazil. We run through a few ongoing cases to explore ways of connecting local work and domestic court proceedings with international activities, especially our transnational lawsuits in Europe or the United States.

The Colombian human rights movement is very active and has successfully won several legal concessions from the state. But the old elites are fighting back, putting obstacles in place wherever they can and relying on violence and corruption to hinder proceedings in Colombian courts. We agree that in the Nestlé case we must exhaust all local remedies and that international legal actions such as compensation claims in the United States and a criminal complaint in Switzerland could then be employed as an effective form of leverage. But the Colombians are skeptical after past experiences with US lawyers who would sweep in domineeringly to gather powers of attorney and witness statements before disappearing back to the United States to file cases there without any further involvement of those affected.

This kind of approach is rejected by all of us as it fails to make the most of self-organization and mobilization inside Colombia. It's clear that those directly affected must be involved in any action we organize in Europe.

We agree that we must take the Nestlé case before Swiss courts. Up to now the position of corporations and government—and many others—is that European standards concerning labor and rights, as well as environmental protection, can be only be upheld in Europe. By this logic, it's none of Europe's business if weak or corrupt governments in Latin America allow commercial activity there to go unregulated. Tightening these laws would threaten jobs and negatively impact the income of European societies in Europe because of the growing price for the outsourced work, according to this argument, and the best way to prevent human rights violations is to rely on voluntary codes. This approach has prevailed for two decades and, as a result, nothing has changed. We want to challenge this position and insist on binding standards and legal liability. The Nestlé case provides a good opportunity to communicate these efforts more widely.

We work on the case with Luciano Romero's family as well as with the trade union and their lawyers. A year and a half later, in December 2011, we have waded through reams of files and witness statements and put together a sound legal argument. Now we need some allies in Geneva, Berne, and Zurich. We find a lawyer in Zurich, longtime leftist advocate Marcel Bosonnet, to represent the claimants before the courts there. We also seek support from NGOs.

This proves to be difficult. Nestlé, Switzerland's flagship firm, conscious of the need to burnish their public standing, are taking part in conferences and discussions. The company recently brought representatives from prominent NGOs on a trip to Colombia before compiling a report with them on the situation there, successfully dampening some of the public criticism of the firm. The murder of Luciano Romero and the threats being made against other trade unionists are mentioned only in passing in the report. The Colombian trade unionists who refused to take part in a dialogue are portrayed as stubborn and dogmatic. The concept of suing companies for human rights violations is new in Switzerland, as in the rest of Europe. For many activists, finding the right balance between dialogue and confrontation is fraught with risk.

In February 2012 ECCHR and its Swiss lawyers, together with Luciana Romero's trade union, file a criminal complaint against Nestlé with prosecutors in the Swiss canton of Zug and present the case at various public events. In Switzerland, Germany, and Austria, the response is huge. The company reacts swiftly but without knowing the legal arguments in the complaint. They think we are repeating an older claim that the firm was directly involved with the murder of Luciano Romero. Since we can't prove that, we've come up with a new legal angle. We argue that the company management knew about the threats against certain workers in Colombia and did nothing, despite repeated calls for help and despite their legal duty to assist. If they had used their influence to intervene, Luciano Romero might still be alive. We aim to establish Nestlé's liability but also to encourage the application of this interpretation of the law to other companies involved in human rights violations outside Europe.

It's the first time a case like this has been submitted in Switzerland and it takes a while before it is taken on board by NGOs and lawyers. The prosecutors in Zug let the case lie on their desks before transferring it to another canton. Their lack of enthusiasm doesn't inspire confidence. Meanwhile, we travel to The Hague with Colombian trade unionists in October 2012 to meet prosecutors from the International Criminal Court. We file a complaint there against Colombian state actors—military and political figures—concerning crimes against humanity related to the persecution of workers. But the preliminary examinations at the court are slow. Colombia, a close ally of the West, manages to appease The Hague prosecutors by initiating domestic investigations, but only against relatively unimportant players. More powerful figures continue to enjoy impunity. Here in The Hague, we see the same double standards we are trying to challenge through our work.

In June 2013 I meet up with trade unionist Javier Correa again in Bogotá. Our friends at the CAJAR lawyers' collective are celebrating twenty-five years of existence—or, perhaps more accurately, survival. Several lawyers have had to go into exile, some have been murdered, all have been placed under constant surveillance, as portrayed in a documentary made about the collective. The film, *Gotas que agrietan la roca,* shows the lawyers going about their daily lives alongside images taken from secret intelligence file photos.

The situation imposes certain restrictions that in turn become virtues: for these lawyers, necessity is the mother of invention. They have put in place flat hierarchies and involve a lot of younger staff in the management. Their structure is decentralized and non-authoritarian, which makes it harder to anticipate their next move and protects them from attack. Some people spend time at CAJAR to gain experience and are then given help to set up their own organizations challenging violence against women, pollution, or other issues. At CAJAR there is none of the egoism that is found in many other groups who are afraid of too much competition, especially for funding.

The activists at CAJAR work closely with affected communities, especially indigenous, black, and rural populations. We meet representatives from the community and hold a role-play exercise based on a land dispute. The lawyer in the role-play, who is supposed to be helping the villagers, is portrayed as badly informed, corrupt, and concerned only with his own interests. This is what the activists have come to expect of our profession. We try to be as open as possible with them but their skepticism is tangible.

And indeed we have little success in the short term. In Switzerland we face defeat after prosecutors in the Nestlé case hold that the claims we are presenting are statute-barred—we should have made the claims earlier, but that was impossible because we didn't have enough knowledge and evidence, a vicious circle. The Colombian trade unionists and lawyers are used to setbacks, but they have other worries. "Will this harm us?" Javier asks me. "Will we face more repression if we lose the case?" The question is justified and very important. Our work is about more than winning in court: through our interventions, we aim to improve the situation for those affected. A basic part of this is ensuring that nothing we do has negative consequences for them. Our Colombian partners have helped us take on a powerful company that has links to violent groups that pose a danger to people on the ground. Local Nestlé representatives have previously falsely accused the trade unionists of being members of the guerrilla, an allegation that can amount to a death sentence. The decision to close the case based on the statute of limitations means at least that they can't claim the allegations have been disproven. And Nestlé does start to budge slightly. For the first time in all the years of dispute, Javier and his colleagues receive an invitation to the Swiss company's headquarters, which they accept.

The bitter truth is that no court—whether in Colombia, Switzerland or anywhere else—is prepared to undertake proper investigations. All we can do is try to work on building publicity around the case. Our campaign does at least lead to a public debate in Switzerland and Germany on the liability of companies in situations of conflict like in Colombia.

Three months earlier, at a café in Manila, I had heard about another murder of a Nestlé trade unionist. In September 2010, the same month that Luciano Romero was killed, Diosdado Fortuna, aka Ka Fort, one of the spokesmen of the long-running strike in a Nestlé plant in the Philippines, was shot by unknown perpetrators riding a motorbike. All the signs, including the place and timing, point to the company's involvement. Shortly before the murder, a military secret service officer was spotted, first in the factory, then hanging around between the police lines, and finally consorting with the strikers. After the murder, angry trade unionists got hold of the man, planning to hand him over to the police. The trade unionists searched his mobile phone and found messages to an unknown person passing on details of Ka Fort's whereabouts. But the suspect was released and received his phone back, and the evidence was never secured. Unlike in the Colombian case, there wasn't even an investigation as to who was the perpetrator.

Now, I'm sitting across the table from Ka Fort's widow and one of his colleagues. I'm furious that we—and the legal system in general—don't have anything more to offer them. We could submit a complaint against the Philippines to the United Nations, but the best we could hope for there would be a response in a few years' time calling on the state to open investigations. And even if this happened, there is very little chance that it would lead to prosecutions of the gunmen or the instigators of the crime. Ka Fort's death is another unresolved case of a murdered activist, and once again it seems Nestlé was involved, but we don't have the evidence needed to take action.

Also present during this discussion is Harry Roque, one of the best-known lawyers in the Philippines and a human rights advocate who was previously involved in proceedings against the former dictator Ferdinand Marcos. Afterward, we drive together to the law faculty at the University of the Philippines where Harry holds a professorship. He has invited me to give a talk about my work, which I have called "From Pinochet to Rumsfeld." There is a lot of interest, especially as to how our approach to law might be employed locally, where the authorities rarely take action on political crimes.

In the future, we hope to look more frequently at human rights violations committed by companies. This is as new for us—lawyers from Berlin, London, and New York—as it is for our partners from the Philippines, Malaysia, Thailand, and Indonesia whom we are meeting up with here in Manila to discuss potential joint projects.

The idea for this kind of exchange came from the Indian lawyer Colin Gonsalves when we met at the previously mentioned conference held in Berlin in autumn 2008. Shortly after the trip to Manila, at a hotel in Delhi, we meet again with Colin, together with his colleagues and a variety of Indian activists. I am aware that India is a country of strong social movements, but I am nonetheless surprised by the sheer momentum of the protests I hear about. There is an impressive array of initiatives but also a lack of political unity and efficacy. The repression the activists face is drastic. Even as we are talking to them about possible legal steps against a huge steelworks in Odisha, the construction of which is linked with widespread forced evictions, news reaches us about the deaths of three activists who had protested against the project. This is the reality of struggle in India. Everyone in the room knows it could just as easily have been them. One man overcomes the dreadful shock of the news and strikes up a defiant song. Everyone else joins in.

Colin got involved in the trade union movement in the seventies while working as an engineer in the textile industry in Bombay. He represented workers in court, even before his increasing political activism led him to study law. In the early eighties, he set up the Human Rights Law Network, which now has over two hundred staff in twenty offices around the country. The organization's biggest victory to date was its right to food case, a public interest litigation action initiated in 2001. Gonsalves and his colleagues argued before the Indian Supreme Court that the deaths of three to five thousand people from starvation each day in India were a breach of the constitutional right to life. The court ruled that there was indeed a right to food and directed the government to set up food programs for around three hundred million people. The decision did not solve the problem of hunger in India, but it did help millions of people.

I go with Colin to visit the Human Rights Law Network at its crowded main offices. As soon as he walks in, he is surrounded: his secretary tries to arrange appointments, his young colleagues come to him for advice, clients appear and want to talk to him. He maintains his calm demeanor, answering all questions with a quiet patience. But it's clear that he can also be very demanding. Anyone who wants to challenge powerful opponents with such limited resources has to be tough, that's his motto.

We gather around a large table. I recount our experiences in Europe, and then Colin's young colleagues describe some of the dramatic conflicts that they have been working on: laws of war in Kashmir, the situation of the Dalit ("untouchable") population, violence against women in all forms, prolonged pre-trial detention, the death penalty, pollution caused by mining. I have never seen such a broad spectrum of work in any other organization. We agree to collaborate more closely in the future. The first step will be to research a project that has long been close to Colin's heart. In Berlin, ECCHR will look into bringing a lawsuit against European companies for serious health problems caused by the use of toxic pesticides. What we are doing here is no less and no more than globalization from below, a new kind of cooperation between lawyers bridging political and cultural differences.

These are my first experiences in Asia. In preparation for the trip I had tried to get a handle on the complexities of the Indian subcontinent's regions, cities, cultures, and religions. It felt overwhelming. The author Ilija Trojanow offered some comfort: "India is constant reminder of how little time one has on this earth," he writes in his book *Gebrauchsanweisung für Indien*. He goes on to quote a guru: "You Westerners want to understand everything because you look with the eyes of the conqueror. But you can't grasp everything. Only an arrogant man tries to understand the whole world. And because he doesn't like to fail, he simplifies the world until he understands it, and everyone does the same thing in their own way." I ask myself if we aren't often guilty of this in our work. Working closely with our partners around the world, I think, might be the only way out of this trap.

***

In the evening of the day after our workshop I arrive at the rail station in Jaipur, a city of three million. There I meet Kavita Srivastava, president of the People's Union for Civil Liberties in Rajasthan. A grayhaired woman in her mid-fifties, she takes charge of the situation immediately. We go to her office, where a lawyer is meeting clients; it's a hive of assistants, volunteers, and people waiting for appointments, all deep in discussion. Kavita bursts into every conversation, introduces me, makes appointments, takes calls on several phones. She shoves me here and there, asks me questions without waiting for an answer. Eventually we drive to her place where her elderly father is having dinner with a friend. When we come in they don't stir, and I feel like I'm intruding. But soon the father sits down beside me and we drink tea. Kavita is on the phone, summoning people; journalists and activists come and go. The next day, my only full day here in Jaipur, had been completely planned out for me. I am due to give a speech at the university, give a press conference, and speak to civil rights activists. I counter that I would also like to see some of the city, and later when a woman and a young man come into the room Kavita breaks off her phone call and shouts at the man, "Are you free tomorrow morning at eight?" His name is Tushar, and he now has the task of taking me on an extensive city tour. The next morning he arrives on his moped to pick me up, and I squeeze on behind him. We drive past the pink buildings in the old town. It's still quiet out. Then we come across a colorful Hindu procession with camels, horses, and vans, all decorated. Flowers are strewn around. We join them for a while before leaving the city and heading out to the great palace at Amber, the historic former regional capital. Here, at the site of so many past wars, fortress walls stretch as far as the eye can see.

We go for a walk under the hot sun and talk. I thought that Tushar was part of the family, but it turns out that the twenty-six-year-old economist works at Kavita's organization. As a Muslim, he has first-hand experience of discrimination. He is married to a Hindu woman, whom I had met the evening before. Before they were married, her parents made life very difficult for him. They reported him to the police and threatened him, and he was forced to leave the city.

In the afternoon it's time to fulfill my duties as guest, and I go to speak at the People's Union for Civil Liberties. The audience includes trade unionists, women's rights activists, and ecologists from all across Rajasthan. They are eager to hear about the Pinochet arrest and our Nestlé case. I also update them on recent developments in our case against Rumsfeld and others concerning US torture. While there are still no significant investigations ongoing, in February 2011 former president George W. Bush canceled a private trip to Switzerland at the last minute because we planned to lodge a criminal complaint and he thought that traveling would be too risky. Most of those present are skeptical. They want to believe me when I say that we can use the law to curb power. But their reality is very different. They invite me to come visit them in their hometowns.

That evening Tushar introduces me to his best friend, a Hindu. We sit drinking beers on the tower of a fort overlooking Jaipur. Tushar's friend is nervous. His family is currently arranging his marriage and, though he is not supposed to, that evening he calls his fiancée several times to talk about their planned trip to Europe. I ask him why a liberal Hindu like him would allow himself to be part of an arranged marriage. They both agree: that's just the way it is in India. The family and the community call the shots; as an individual, there's nothing you can do to change this. I argue that Tushar proved you could do it differently. They disagree. Only in Bombay are things open enough for this. Everywhere else there would be problems, they say, families and villages chase down any renegades, following them to the cities. After a while, I stop asking about it. On the way home in the car, we listen to Hindu pop turned up loud.

***

Three days later I fly to China, arriving in hypermodern Beijing. Rem Koolhaas and other architects have left their mark on the city; their buildings stand side by side with the ancient palaces. The contrast with Delhi couldn't be more pronounced, and the comparison of the two helps me understand both cities better. I am scheduled to give two lectures at Beijing University. The campus, the buildings, the lecture halls, the cafeteria, the lattes, large, small, double shot—this could be anywhere in the world. It is Saturday afternoon and the students are tired. Some lay their heads on their desks and go to sleep. They have a full timetable of lectures and have been at university since early morning.

Again I talk about the development of international criminal law, the Pinochet case, Rumsfeld, and Guantánamo. I know that this university is a liberal bastion, but I'm still somewhat surprised. The discussion is lively; many students ask about the role of corporations in human rights violations. The topic of human rights violations in China hangs in the air; some people address it directly. One woman in the audience, for instance, works on the lack of rights of the country's two hundred million migrant workers. I had given some thought beforehand to what I could or should say publicly in China, but the discussion is much the same as it would be in Stockholm or Barcelona.

***

Colombia, the Philippines, India, China—the journeys and encounters along the way have presented me with a host of new and somewhat overwhelming impressions. I'm able to bring these experiences into the debate and gain some new insights. I am moved by the presence of a new generation of lawyers, young men and a striking number of young women, from different milieus and cultures. They are free from the paternalism of the older human rights crowd. Instead of taking a "top-down" approach, working from the West or their big cities, they work with the affected communities as a matter of course. It is heartening to know that they will bring new momentum to human rights litigation in the coming years.

Alejandra Ancheita from Mexico is a good example of this new kind of political lawyer. We've been friends for many years, and I've always been impressed by her stringent seriousness. This might be due to her own personal history. At a young age, Alejandra learned about the high human cost that often goes hand in hand with human rights work in Mexico. Her father, who fought to secure the rights of workers and indigenous people, was found dead on Alejandra's eighth birthday.

Her mentor, environmental lawyer Digna Ochoa, was murdered in October 2001. Both had clearly crossed paths with some very powerful interests.

For decades the Mexican state presented a progressive facade to the world, concealing the fact that the country was engaged in the same kind of dirty war against oppositionists as was going on in many South American states. A continuous thread runs from the Tlatelolco massacre on October 2, 1968, to the disappearance of forty-three trainee teachers in Ayotzinapa in spring 2014.

In 2005 Alejandra set up ProDESC, an organization that endeavors to protect the economic, social, and cultural rights of the marginalized in Mexico, work which often brings them into conflict with transnational corporations, mining companies, and landowners. Over the years she has on several occasions had to leave the country because her life was at risk. Each time she has returned to continue her work.

In September 2014 I'm in Geneva to see Alejandra accept the Martin Ennals Award, a prestigious European human rights prize. There are over five hundred guests at the ceremony. The atmosphere is formal, the evening impeccably organized. A short film about Alejandra and her work is screened. Her fighting spirit is evident throughout. In one scene that echoes Hannah Arendt's dictum on the enforcement of the right to rights, Alejandra speaks in front of a group of indigenous people whose property rights were breached. She talks forcibly to them: "These are your rights, they are set down in the laws of this country. This isn't a gift to you, you're entitled to it. It will not be easy, but we can win." This is the attitude she radiates: the fight isn't easy, but we can win.

It's just after the prize-giving ceremony and Alejandra and I are sitting in a Geneva bistro. I try to draw her out a bit: "Why didn't you ask all those people in the audience if, on your next visit to Switzerland, they would give you an equally warm welcome if you had a criminal complaint against a Swiss company in your hand?"

With a serious look she turns to me and says, "Because, my dear, that's your job. For me this prize means protection. It gives me the backing of the European human rights establishment and more of a public profile. You're the one who has to argue with the Europeans."

Instead I prefer to ask: is it really hope, that which can never end in disappointment? Hope implies that it might bring disappointment, that it will bring disappointment, because hope is not the same as sureness—it is wrapped up in danger and in the fact that things might also be different.

... Nothing is certain or settled, things are still in development. We are heading toward an unknown land, a land that has yet to come into existence in fact, a place just beginning to emerge from the sea of possibilities we are entering—entering as wanderers and as the compass and as the land itself, all at once.

Hope entails being disappointed, but it also entails making adjustments and corrections as we go along, otherwise we would end up in a fool's paradise. That would be an abstract utopia, something that is dreamed up or tested only in one's mind. ... That is why one must look closely at where the thing is headed. Adjustments and corrections can come only from a considered, justified hope, not from the fool's paradise. ... From this fool's paradise can come no real criticism, only bluster and ranting.

Ernst Bloch, *Gespräche mit Ernst Bloch*

EPILOGUE: JUSTIFIED HOPE

Sometimes I feel like the wandering Chilean in Roberto Bolaño's story "Mauricio ("The Eye") Silva." I cry, I feel powerless and infinitely angry. But then I meet one of the many people pursuing the same struggle in their countries. And I laugh. I laugh as I write the stories in this book, and look forward to the next time I will see those who feature in them. This alone makes it all worthwhile.

It's a balmy summer's night in early 2015, and I'm sitting with David Campora, an eighty-one-year-old ex-guerrillero and expert on the revolutionary movements. We are in his garden in Montevideo—a few blocks from the house where he cooked up my first ever *asado*. He's currently reading a book called *No hay mañana sin ayer—Without Yesterday There Is No Tomorrow*. That's your area, he says with a smile. He's proud of what has been achieved in his country, where his party colleague and former prison mate Pepe Mujica is currently president: "In Uruguay, we've built a structurally left-wing majority and a stable progressive project. Not bad for our little country, given the state of the world." He has bequeathed his private archive on the history of the Tupamaros to a university library.

At a party at Betina Ehrenhaus' place in Buenos Aires I meet Mariana, Lorena, Cristina, Rodolfo, and others. Once again I have heated discussions about Peronism with Marcelo von Schmeling, whose sister and father were disappeared. As a political functionary,

Marcelo has stayed loyal to this odd collective of a movement that includes revolutionaries, like his disappeared relatives, in addition to many right-wingers. Marcelo keeps referring to *la nación*, the nation, and *el pueblo*, the people, and with a rising anger, I remind him how the nationalists on the Right also use these categories. Then we started reminiscing about Ellen Marx. He tells of how she would plead with him for hours on end to convince him that he and his generation had to continue the fight for justice.

At a corner café, I meet the Mercedes trade unionist Héctor Ratto, now sixty-five. His haggard face bears the marks of a hard day at work and a long working life, during which his commitment to the cause led to his torture and imprisonment. He is pleased that his three daughters managed to climb the social ladder; one is a copywriter, one an accountant, and the third a psychologist. He never had high hopes for the legal proceedings against Mercedes. "The corporation is too powerful, the government always stepped in to help them." That's why we haven't won any of the legal battles up to now, he says. Yet he's not frustrated about our efforts over the last fifteen years. "If you never try, then you never even have a chance." The legal action did at least lead to books, articles, and films being produced about the repression faced by him and his colleagues, he says matter-of-factly. I am glad to see Héctor. He is a politically aware worker who doesn't need to have the world explained to him by someone like me. And yet the reunion leaves a bitter aftertaste. His pension is not enough, and he still has to work at an engineering factory in Villa Urquiza. Meanwhile, I travel all over the world, living in comparative comfort. The gulf between lawyers like me and so many of those we represent is one of the biggest contradictions of our work. Merely being aware of this problem—is that enough?

Adriana Marcus left behind the human rights scene in Buenos Aires long ago and has become even more forceful in her criticism. We're sitting in front of her wooden house in the middle of a small Patagonian forest surrounded by primeval trees like the *arrayán* and the *coihue*. "They talk about nothing else, it's not healthy. I'm more than an ESMA survivor, I'm also a mother, wife, aunt, daughter, partner, doctor, and gardener." Yet she still travels to Buenos Aires, a day's journey away, to give testimony in the court proceedings. She takes a nuanced view of the potential of the criminal law. For her, it's not primarily about seeing someone convicted and locked away for the rest of his life. She is not looking for any simple solutions. "What I want is for some state authority, the judiciary, to publicly acknowledge that what I am saying is true." She also wants to not have to meet the men from the military, her old torturers, on the street. Above all, though, she says society has to address the lasting consequences of these crimes. She's worried about the next generation because she sees children and grandchildren suffering from the effects of the torture. She tells me about young women who were born in prison after their mothers were raped and tortured with electric shocks and who are now suffering from serious health and emotional problems.

I've always got on famously with Raúl Montenegro, environmental activist and winner of the alternative Nobel Prize. At a lunch in Buenos Aires, Raúl describes our affinity as the product of a convergent cultural evolution: just as different species living in distant places in very different ecosystems sometimes develop uncanny similarities, our own experiences have led us both to remarkably similar conclusions. We talk about our work, about triumphs and defeats. Both, he says, are part of the same evolutionary process. Both are essential for the formation of adaptive capabilities in complex social systems. This is the only way we can develop resilience. The kind of thinking that would bluntly classify things simply as successes or failures is alien to us both. We have to accept the possibility of failure, to address it productively, analyze it, and adjust our strategies accordingly. The threat of failure does not justify inaction, especially when action can improve matters, and defeat won't cause any lasting damage. These small steps forward should be acknowledged. I believe in this tangible utopia, this other aesthetic of resistance, and yet I still ask myself if by doing so we are glossing over the underlying, deep-rooted power structures. I tell him that I sometimes think we are acting as a major employment scheme for lawyers and PR experts in companies whose job it is to co-opt our discourse and show that they've taken the necessary precautions to avoid any human rights violations. Raúl and his young daughter burst out laughing.

I've been seeing Michael Ratner more often since he started representing WikiLeaks head Julian Assange and making regular visits to him at the Ecuadorian embassy in London. Michael laments how little has changed politically since President Obama took office in January 2009. Every so often we'll argue because I find that his work is too much focused on rights violations in the United States. "But it's my country and it's my government, I have to do something about it," he counters. I've visited Assange in the embassy a number of times and it's difficult to properly appreciate the situation he's in and the dangers he faces. It's difficult to accept that in terrorism trials in the United States and the United Kingdom, secrecy prevails to the same devastating degree as experienced by K. in Kafka's *The Trial*: the suspects never know the charges against them and as a result cannot properly defend themselves. The concept of a fair trial was once the cornerstone of Anglo-American legal culture. Now, anti-terrorism laws are being interpreted so broadly as to encompass even the revelations from Chelsea Manning, Assange, and Snowden. It is nightmarish to read a legal opinion from US lawyers in which a life sentence for espionage is set out as a realistic prospect for Edward Snowden.

It's March 2015 and I've just cooked dinner for Michael. After we eat, I read some of my assessments of our work from the manuscript of this book. He keeps interrupting and telling me I need to put more emphasis on the positive developments. He shares my view that if you look back over the last fifteen years, a clear pattern emerges: from absolute impunity—for dictators like Ríos Montt, Jorge Videla, and Charles Taylor—toward a legal accountability, increasingly also for powerful actors. He is pleased to hear that the German federal prosecution authorities in Karlsruhe have been restructured to allow them to pursue crimes against international law. For now, most of the prosecutors are working exclusively on Rwanda and Congo, but at least the investigators have started implementing something we've been advocating for the past ten years: specialized bodies gathering evidence, witness testimony, and documentation. We were of course particularly pleased when the Germans opened preliminary investigations in December 2014 after the release of the Senate report on CIA torture.

Does this mean that all is well? Of course not. But there is noticeable progress that we could not necessarily have anticipated. For years we worked away at this. It was not in vain.

***

Peter Weiss takes it one step further, as always. In a French bistro on New York's Upper West Side, he asks me how our US torture cases are going. He's no longer very optimistic about the implementation of universal jurisdiction; he says he won't be around to see it happen. But when the conversation turns to the topic closest to his heart, Peter, who is at this point eighty-nine and has difficulty hearing and seeing, says he is still fighting for a world free of atomic weapons.

In autumn 1990, as Germany reunification was underway, I was at the Guatemalan Human Rights Commission in Mexico getting my first experience in human rights work. At the time I found it hard to imagine that I could ever work in Europe and be as useful to the human rights struggle as those people who were working in the Commission to ensure they could one day return to a democracy in their home country. In Guatemala, I meet Anantonia Reyes, who was head of the Commission at that time. She was able to return after the peace agreement in 1996 and continue the academic career she'd had to abandon while in exile. Now she's teaching at the university and working for the state human rights body, once notorious for its proximity to the regime.

It's a moving encounter with Anantonia. We compare notes on what has happened over the past twenty-five years, and we see we've traveled somewhat parallel paths. Former dictator Ríos Montt, who remained firmly in power in 1990, was since convicted of genocide. Even in Guatemala things have changed. And then again, not so much. Indigenous politicians in the Guatemalan highlands are facing harassment and threats for organizing opposition to mining and infrastructure projects. Yet the fact that it is possible to take action within global networks in the fight for human rights and thus ensure that ever fewer crimes remain invisible—this is perhaps our greatest success.

Nothing is past—not for me and not for those I encountered on this journey. The conversation I've been having with them, and with myself, will continue—and so will our work. This is a story with no end.

FURTHER READING

In this book I wanted to set out my—and our—work in a way that is different from my usual approach. For readers interested in learning more about the themes in the book, below are some recommended texts. Many of the works are in German, with the English version given when available.

The torture allegations against the United Kingdom along with several other issues arising in this text are set out on the ECCHR website (www.ecchr.eu). *A Very British Killing* by A. T. Williams provides a good but harrowing account of the death of Baha Mousa in Iraq. The double standards in international criminal law are addressed in my own book *Double Standards: International Criminal Law and the West*. Anyone who hasn't yet seen Laura Poitras's film *Citizenfour* or read Glenn Greenwald's book *No Place to Hide* should do so.

Some of the many books that made an impression on me during my studies: *Hitler's Justice: the Courts of the Third Reich* by Ingo Müller, *The Brief Summer of Anarchy* by Hans Magnus Enzensberger, and *The Investigation* by Peter Weiss. David Campora is someone you just have to meet, but as something of a substitute you can read his memories of his time in detention as put down on paper by Ernesto González Bermejo in *Las manos en el fuego*.

My big trip was inspired by Bruce Chatwin's *In Patagonia*. In *The Songlines*, he sets out his ideas about a person who is born a nomad.

He makes frequent reference to Osvaldo Bayer's standard work, *La Patagonia Rebelde* (*Rebellion in Patagonia*). In his book *Lebenswege*, my friend Gert Eisenbürger describes fifteen biographies between Europe and Latin America, including that of Pieter Siemsen, who late in life published his autobiography under the title *Der Lebensanfänger: Erinnerungen eines anderen Deutschen.*

Erich Hackl not only gave me ongoing encouragement to write, he also published important books like *Sara und Simón*, about a Uruguayan mother's search for her kidnapped son.

The Truth Commission report *Nunca más* (available in English under the title *Never Again: Report of Conadep* [National Commission on the Disappearance of Persons]) offers an authentic insight into the horrors of Argentina's military dictatorship. In *Kampf gegen die Straflosigkeit: Argentiniens Militärs vor Gericht*, I sought to summarize my own thoughts on the matter. Jeanette Erazo Heufelder wrote the book I always wanted to write: a moving biography of Ellen Marx called *Von Berlin nach Buenos Aires.*

Gaby Weber published her research on the disappeared of Mercedes-Benz in book form in *Die Verschwundenen von Mercedes-Benz*. Konstantin Thun, who left this world much too young, takes a critical look at West German foreign policy in *Menschenrechte und Außenpolitik: Bundesrepublik Deutschland—Argentinien 1976–1983,* as does Frieder O. Wagner in his films *Todesursache Schweigen* and *Dass du zwei Tage schweigst unter der Folter!*, which were released with accompanying texts in the Bibliothek des Widerstands series by the Laika publishing house. The Colectivo Situaciones have published a small manifesto on the escrache actions as a form of resistance.

Marcelo Brodsky's photographic essay "Buena Memoria" can be found in various languages. The catalogs from the two exhibitions with Eduardo Molinari and others in Berlin (*Alltag und Vergessen: Argentinien*

1976/2003) and Cologne (*Ex Argentina: Schritte zur Flucht von der Arbeit zum Tun*) can still be found in good art bookshops in Germany. Mariana Corral's life story is told by Sebastián Hacher in *Cómo enterrar a un padre desaparecido.*

A lot of interesting work has been published in recent years by the critical postcolonial writers from the TWAIL (Third World Approaches to International Law) school. Standout texts include Makau Mutua's *Savages, Victims and Saviors* and Tshepo Madlingozi's *On Transitional Justice Entrepreneurs and the Production of Victims.*

A number of books and films have emerged addressing the torture that began after 9/11, including Alfred McCoy's *A Question of Torture: CIA Interrogation, from the Cold War to the War on Terror* and Jan Philipp Reemtsma's *Folter im Rechtsstaat?* In *Chain of Command*, Seymour Hersh gives an overview of how the Bush administration conspired to break the law. Guantánamo survivor Murat Kurnaz gives a harrowing account of his experiences in *Five Years of My Life: An Innocent Man in Guantanamo.* Powerful films on the topic include Alex Gibney's *Taxi to the Dark Side*, on the torture and murder of a young Afghani man, and two works by Errol Morris: *Standard Operating Procedure* on the photos of abuse at Abu Ghraib, and *The Unknown Known*, a portrait of Donald Rumsfeld that also addresses the case of Mohammad al-Qahtani.

More information on our human rights litigation against corporations—which was still in its initial stages when this book was written—can be found on the ECCHR website. See for example the litigation brought in Germany against German clothing retailer KiK in connection with a September 2012 fire at its supplier factory in Pakistan that killed over 250 people.

ACKNOWLEDGMENTS

Lawyers and social movements around the world use the law to challenge human rights violations. The work is done in teams and through networks of which I feel I am part. Over the years I have been lucky enough to work with so many dedicated and passionate people; it would be impossible to list them all here. This includes people directly affected by torture, detention, loss, and injustice: in particular, I have learned a great deal from Ellen Marx. Thanks to Gert Eisenbürger and Danuta Sacher, my colleagues at RAV; my colleagues at the law firm Hummel/Kaleck: Dieter Hummel, Volker Ratzmann, Martin Rubbert, Klaus Piegeler, Mechtild Kuby, Sönke Hilbrans, Peer Stolle, Sebastian Scharmer, Jacqueline Schröder, Jenny Göppert, and Melanie Nemsow; those at the Coalition Against Impunity: Angelika Denzler, Esteban Cuya, Mechthild Baum, Jan Dunkhorst, Roland Beckert, and others; all the staff at the European Center for Constitutional and Human Rights, especially Albert Koncsek and Miriam Saage-Maaß, Andreas Schüller, Anabel Bermejo, Yvonne Veith, Carsten Gericke, Marie Badarne, Claire Tixeire, Carolijn Terwindt, Hanaa Hakiki and Claudia Müller-Hoff, and Erwin Single for the initial push. Without you, this work, which is so important for me, would not be possible.

While working on this text, I met up with many of the people who feature in it, in Montevideo and Buenos Aires, in Berlin and New York, Mexico and Guatemala. Adriana Marcus, Peter Weiss, and Michael

Ratner read and commented on entire chapters; I also spoke with Julia Littmann, David Campora, Rodolfo Yanzon and Marcelo Brodsky, Eduardo Molinari, Lorena Bossi, Mariana Corral, Héctor Ratto, Marcelo von Schmeling, Anantonia Reyes, Alejandra Ancheita, Isha Khandelwal, Kranti Chinnappa, Lotte Leicht, Reed Brody, Vince Warren, and Baher Azmy, furthering the conversations we've been having for so many years. I hope that they can recognize something of themselves in these stories.

The idea for this book came from Jen Robinson, Matthias Landwehr, and Frank Jakobs. I thank Julia Prosinger, the first person to read the manuscript, for her valuable critique and comments, as well as Albert Koncsek, Bernd Müssig, Carsten Gericke, Lena Kampf, and Naomi Hennig. My thanks go also to Irene Sinigaglia, who saw a book of Bruce Chatwin's letters on my desk and said, "You are different from him. On each of your trips, you leave behind a piece of yourself." And to Chowra Makaremi, who urged me to free myself from both narcissism and shame while writing in the first person.

For the German version of this book, I thank Karsten Kredel from Hanser Berlin and his colleagues, especially Ludger Ikas and Thomas Rohde, for the faith and commitment they placed in this book.

***

And for the English version, a big thanks goes to Colin Robinson and OR Books for their support from the first moment they heard about the project. I also want to thank Tony Tabatznik, who encouraged me and supported its publication. His perspective encouraged me to see the book partly as a way to communicate with the lawyers—both those younger and more experienced—in the Bertha Foundation Justice Initiative about how to challenge political and economic power with legal means.